Wilfred Burchett, the well-known Australian journalist, was the first Western correspondent into Hiroshima in 1945 and his historic exclusive report on what he saw appeared in the London *Daily Express* in September of that year. Later he reported the Korean peace talks from the North Korean side for *Ce Soir*. He began reporting the Vietnam War in 1963 for the Japanese Mainichi group, the British *Morning Star* and the American *National Guardian* working from Hanoi. Dressed in typical Vietnamese pyjamas and conical straw hat, he travelled for hundreds of miles throughout North and South Vietnam, mainly on foot or by bicycle, on horseback or by motorized sampan. Despite his obvious support for the Vietcong he was asked by Henry Kissinger to serve as a go-between for the United States at Hanoi. He now lives in Paris.

ALSO BY WILFRED BURCHETT
Pacific Treasure Island
Bombs over Burma
Wingate Adventure
Democracy with a Tommy-Gun
Cold War in Germany
People's Democracies
The Changing Tide [play]
China's Feet Unbound
This Monstrous War
Koje Unscreened [with Alan Winnington]
Plain Perfidy [with Alan Winnington]
North of the 17th Parallel
Mekong Upstream
Come East Young Man
The Furtive War: The United States in Viet Nam and Laos
My Visit to the Liberated Zones of South Viet Nam
Viet Nam: Inside Story of the Guerilla War
Viet Nam North
Viet Nam Will Win
Again Korea
Passport
The Second Indochina War
My War with the CIA [with Prince Norodom Sihanouk]
Portugal After the Captains' Coup
China: The Quality of Life [with Rewi Alley]
Grasshoppers and Elephants
The Whores of War

To Comrade and Sigmund with my deepest affection cemented by all the things that

CATAPULT TO FREEDOM

we all believe in.

Wilfred

WILFRED BURCHETT

25/8/1978

QUARTET BOOKS
LONDON MELBOURNE NEW YORK

First published by Quartet Books Limited 1978
A member of the Namara Group
27 Goodge Street, London W1P 1FD

Copyright © 1978 by Wilfred Burchett

ISBN 0 7043 2156 4

Typeset by Bedford Typesetters Ltd
Printed in Great Britain by litho at The Anchor Press Ltd
and bound by Wm Brendon & Son Ltd
both of Tiptree, Essex

CONTENTS

LIST OF ILLUSTRATIONS

FOREWORD

I have had the good luck to know Wilfred Burchett off and on (more often off than on, such is the vagrant nature of our trade) ever since we toiled together – most improbably, when you think of it – in the Fleet Street vineyard of the Chateau Beaverbrook. We abandoned this patronage and the *Express* at almost exactly the same time, though for marginally different reasons.

To his dying day, which took a long time to come, the Lord believed that our defections had been politically coordinated; he was, as so often, quite wrong. In fact at the time I had never even met Wilfred. Indeed I did not know his name was Wilfred. As an Australian he worked for the *Express* during the war in the Pacific; I was in Asia and Europe. He signed his file simply: Burchett. They had to find an acceptable byline for this gifted but remote correspondent, so someone or other arbitrarily called him 'Peter'. Fleet Street was always pretty cavalier about identities. Nevertheless, for some time after I established a kinship for this wayward old mate I had a job unscrambling the Peter from the real man. And it is a real man.

We met briefly in the post-war Balkans; neither he nor I for the life of us can remember where, or why. When I made one of the early and tentative visits to China in the 50s he was there to greet me and to let me lean on him professionally in friendship and the common frustrations of our preposterous reporters' job. In those days Wilfred seemed to be a committed Communist, I was not; I still had some doctrinal reservations that were not, I think, wholly ignoble. I respected Wilfred, he respected me. This has never changed. The things we share are far more than those on which we differ, and the gap diminishes.

What we shared then, and still do, is an enduring interest in and affection for South-East Asia, and of course especially for Vietnam, and this book is about Vietnam. Wilfred Burchett knows that lovely obstinate tragic country a thousand times better than I; he lived there longer and travelled farther. I know it in an oblique and probably superficial way, far less than Burchett but nevertheless perhaps a little more than most *chers collegues* from the late Press Center in Saigon. I was there in the French days before Dien Bien Phu – attached, God help me, to the Foreign Legion, in a company that appeared to be composed entirely of minor German war criminals on the run and that was commanded by an officer with the almost totally unbelievable name of Capitaine La Trine. I saw the French leave and the Americans arrive; one *mission civilatrice* replacing another, with an irony we could not appreciate at the time.

During the height of the American war I managed in a very awkward and circuitous way to get myself into Hanoi and most of the North, which was to say the least unusual at the time. The idea was to write and film something to support my thesis that the North of Vietnam was peopled by recognizable human beings and not devils incarnate with horns and tails. This, needless to say, got me no hosannahs in the United States, indeed very much otherwise. That was until the American tide turned and what had been sedition turned abruptly into sense. It became, quite suddenly, respectable to demand peace.

Wilfred Burchett's book is not the story of those last few ugly years; there have been plenty of them. I have about twenty-five myself. Hardly any of them even start to examine what the Vietnamese people *are*, where they come from,

what over the centuries has made this little nation so tenaciously, enduringly, stubbornly resistant to foreign threats
and incursions, long before the French, long before the
Americans. How did this small and seemingly gentle people
retain a positive identity for so long, even to the extent of
defeating at last the most powerful military enterprise in the
world?

This is where I disagree with Wilfred Burchett's title:
Catapult to Freedom, which suggests a sudden and immediate
acceleration of endeavour, a compulsive response to aggression. He himself defines how long the process has continued,
for centuries before the American B52s, centuries before Dien
Bien Phu. The whole theme of Wilfred's book is that Vietnam
did not catapult; Vietnam endured. It endured because the
Vietnamese intuitively knew that their personal self – socially,
politically, aesthetically, culturally, even genetically – had an
inalienable right to independence, and in the end they proved
their point.

This book explains so much of the shadows of Vietnam's
history that I did not know, that almost certainly no French
legionary knew, that without doubt none of the baffled and
brutal and often despairing GIs ever knew, and that I
would suppose very few ordinary Vietnamese ever knew. The
research involved would have daunted anyone but brother
Burchett, but he knew it had to be done.

To the outside world the architect of modern Vietnam was
the wry and scholarly Nguyen Ai Quoc, who came to be known
as Ho Chi Minh, a man of parts if ever there was one. Wilfred
Burchett talked with him in 1954; it was a full ten years later
that I met him, in Hanoi. During all my uneasy stay there the
President had refused even to see me; he had not been visible
for months; I began to wonder if the rumours were true that
he was in fact dead. I knew of his extraordinary eclectic
record – poet, patriot, politician, strategist, revolutionary,
philosopher, his exile in France, even his apprenticeship to
Escoffier as pastrycook at the Carlton Hotel in the Haymarket
in London. I very much hoped he was not dead.

Then one day I was asked for a drink by the Prime
Minister, Pham Van Dong. After a long session I became

aware that Uncle Ho had joined us, silently arriving in his Vietnamese rubber-tyre sandals, unannounced. He said: 'No talk about politics, right? You've had three hours with my Prime Minister; that ought to be enough even for you. Tell me, what is the Haymarket like these days?'

I had to say that the old Carlton had been demolished. 'Like so much else,' he said. Then: 'May we converse in English? These days I get little opportunity to practise.' For a while we tried, but he was very rusty; we reverted to French.

I wish Ho Chi Minh had lived; he was the one Communist head of state I ever met with a bubbling sense of humour, a wicked wit; he was the only one in my experience who could make jokes about the Party. Was Uncle Ho a Communist who became a freedom-fighter, or was he a Vietnamese patriot who became a Communist because the Communists were the only people who appeared to care about freedom? I shall never know, because all we talked of was how, at the height of the American war, we were smoking Camel cigarettes and drinking Schlitz beer. And I never got the answer to that either.

This is a frivolous end to an introduction to a book of serious and absorbing scholarship, but Wilfred knows me enough to forgive me. Indeed he may well have told me the tale in the first place.

If anyone expects from this book a polemic, a pamphlet on contemporary issues, this is not the volume for him. This is a record, and indeed the only one I know, of the part this graceful and inflexible little nation has played in the pageant of Asian history: the symbol of an unconquerable survival.

JAMES CAMERON
November 1977

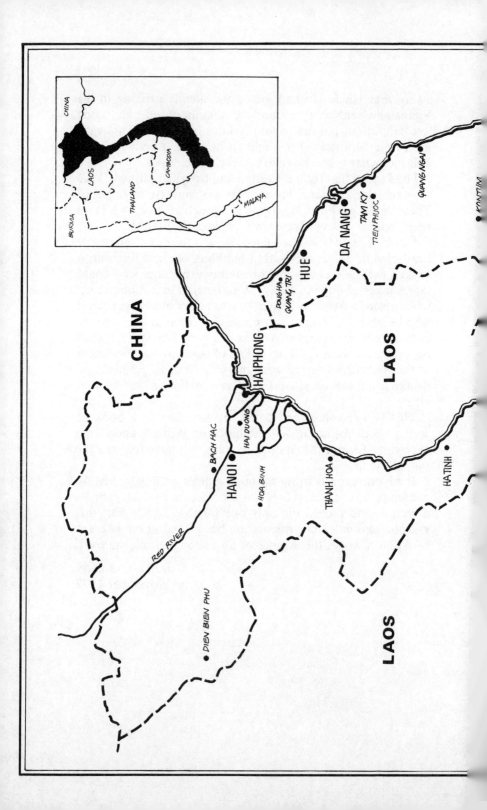

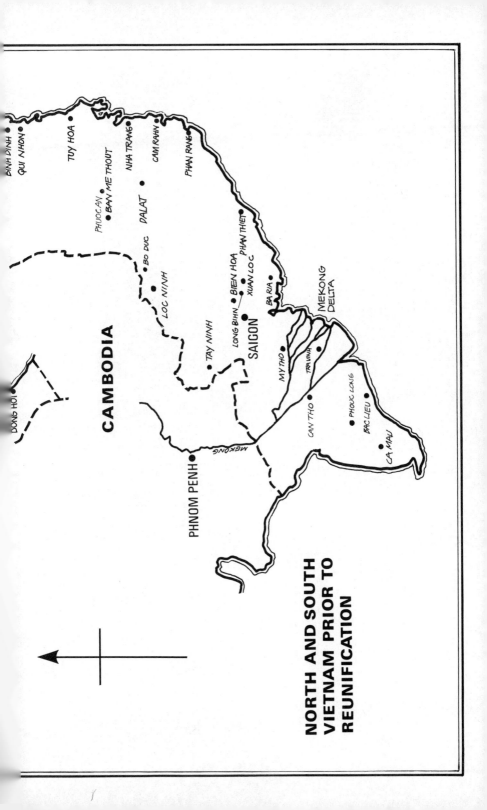

NORTH AND SOUTH
VIETNAM PRIOR TO
REUNIFICATION

CAMBODIA

PHNOM PENH

MEKONG

MEKONG
DELTA

SAIGON

DONG HOI

BINH DINH
QUI NHON
TUY HOA
BAN ME THOUT
PHUOC AN
NHA TRANG
CAM RANH
DALAT
PHAN RANG
BO DUC
LOC NINH
PHAN THIET
XUAN LOC
BIEN HOA
LONG BINH
BA RIA
TAY NINH
MY THO
TRA VINH
CAN THO
PHUOC LONG
BAC LIEU
CA MAU

INTRODUCTION

Who are these people who have dared to stand up to the mightiest powers of their day for the past 2000 years, always cocksure that they would come off the winners? It is a question that has concerned me ever since 10 October 1954, when I caught up with vanguard units of the Vietnam People's Army (VPA) as they were about to take over Hanoi from retreating units of the French Expeditionary Force. It was my first sight of the regular forces of both sides.

My first impression of the VPA troops was how small and boyish they seemed. How trim and neat in their well-washed khaki cottons and rubber-tyred sandals. Relaxed, smiling, wisecracking with each other as they awaited the word to move on, capable of a sudden switch to discipline at a soft-spoken command. Grenades in cloth waist belts, American carbines (captured by the Chinese in Korea I was later to discover) and a few light machine-guns. Everything light and functional, the atmosphere informal. Suitable for the world's most nimble foot soldiers.

What a contrast to the French troops, many of them black African giants, moving back as the VPA moved forward according to the agreed takeover procedure. Tanks and armoured cars, artillery, troops in heavy uniforms, soggy with sweat – dirty, exhausted men, piling into lines of ten-wheeled trucks, seemingly crushed between steel helmets and heavy ankle boots.

In innumerable visits to Vietnam since, including a period of residence in Hanoi for nearly three years, plus some on-the-spot observation of how similar boyish types in rubber sandals were standing up to the American forces in South Vietnam, the question as to why the Vietnamese are as they are was posed with ever greater insistence. It hammered away not only at my consciousness but at that of editors, publishers and public, demanding deeper explanations than those of military, political and organizational factors.

Even a superficial glance at Vietnamese history shows that they have been standing up to powers infinitely greater than themselves for over 2000 years. The Chinese in their heyday of expansion conquered all the 'barbarian' tribes south of the Yangtze river, known to them as the Bac Viet (Hundred Viets). All, that is, except the Viet Lac, who lived in what later became known as North Vietnam. The *lac* characterization refers to a long-tailed sea bird of that name found on early bronze and ceramic relics, which this obstinate collection of tribes adopted as their emblem. It was not just the latter-day French and Americans who found the Viet Lac difficult to subdue! However, after occupying Vietnam for about 1000 trouble-filled years, the Chinese were thrown out in the tenth century and over fifty subsequent invasions were all eventually repelled.

The Mongols of Genghis and Kublai Khan, whose 'Golden Hordes' conquered most of the known world of their time, came to grief, too, in three attempts to subjugate the Viet Lac. These were not small affairs but involved up to 500,000 Mongol warriors. The last defeat which could justifiably be called one of the decisive battles of world history, sent the Mongol empire into its decline.

In more recent times, Siamese invaders in the late eighteenth century, despite shorter supply lines and an invitation to invade from the reigning Vietnamese monarch, fared no better than the Chinese or Mongols. A few decades later the French were more successful – but finally only one tenth as successful as the Chinese – staying less than a century. The Americans did

2

about one twentieth as well as the French, maintaining their presence in half the country for less than ten years.

What is their secret? During the past century western ethnologists, archaeologists, historians, social scientists, psychiatrists and others, have been busy explaining about the Vietnamese. Their most valid Vietnamese counterparts were too busy fighting wars, languishing in prisons or uprooted in exile, to have their say. Those that survived are now diligently at work, discovering their past, delving into the origins of the extraordinary tenacity and vitality of their people. They are generous in sharing their discoveries with outsiders who share their interest.

The overall question is simple. How have the Vietnamese not only managed to defend their territory for over 2000 years, but to defend their way of life, their language, their own distinctive psychology, humour and way of thinking? Why were they the one group of Viets among a hundred who were not assimilated?

If the question is simple, the reply has to be long and complex. In scores of conversations with Vietnamese leaders, including Ho Chi Minh, Pham Van Dong, Vo Nguyen Giap, Ton Duc Thang, Van Tien Dung (the commander of the last great campaign), scientists, writers and others, when I have probed their views for the secret of their survival and victories, the replies could be summed up as: 'Ah, to understand that you would have to go deeply into our history, our literature, our poetry, discover our soul and that is impossible for an outsider.'

It is thus with considerable diffidence that I have yielded to a publisher's request to supply the elements of an answer. As a non-specialist in almost all the subjects covered – except that of knowing the Vietnamese people, their leaders and how they fight and work – I have relied heavily on recognized Vietnamese specialists and on increasingly available translations of Vietnamese literature and documentation, in dealing with the various aspects covered.

Why the Vietnamese always win can never be explained by an analysis of military strategies and tactics alone. The deeper one probes the more evident this becomes.

When I put the question to General Van Tien Dung, the field commander of what is called for short 'The 1975 Spring Offensive', as to what extent the strategies and tactics employed were influenced by those of the great battles throughout Vietnam's history, he replied: 'But this was the great culmination of the experiences of all the battles fought by our ancestors.'

CHAPTER 1

BACK TO THE ORIGINS

There have been many hypotheses as to where the Vietnamese originated. Some French teachers, whose patriotic fervour outweighed their scientific objectivity, taught Vietnamese children that their ancestors were from migratory tribes related to the Gauls. Modern Vietnamese believe they were always there and that they descended from their own apes, had their own 'Peking Man', and if they did not have a Neanderthal Man, this was because he was a deviation in the development of *Homo sapiens* which they could well do without. Plenty of migratory tribes drifted into Vietnam but were grafted onto the original stock which was non-migratory. For a more scientific view I sought out Professor Pham Huy Thong, a Vietnamese archaeologist who had worked with France's prestigious CNSR (National Council of Scientific Research), and who is now Director of Vietnam's Institute of Archaeology and Vice-President of the State Committee for Social Sciences. A small, shy, bespectacled person, Pham Huy Thong epitomizes the traditional Vietnamese scholar-patriot, combining modesty and courage. I already knew that hardly had the smoke cleared away from the battle at Xuan Loc – the fiercest of the war which opened the gates to Saigon – than Pham Huy Thong was there on the track of some new archaeological finds. 'Every country is interested in its own past. We think that discoveries throwing light on this exalts and develops sentiments of national pride.' He was obviously passionately pleased to be back at his own speciality. 'Where were Vietnamese archaeologists in this quest to discover their own origins?' I asked.

There is still a lot we don't know but at least we know far more than we did twenty years ago. The French knew of the vestiges of what is known as the Hoa Binh Man, dating back 4000 years, but they thought 5000 to 6000 years was the maximum to place the existence of primitive man in Vietnam. We have found more evidence of Neolithic Man around Hoa Binh and elsewhere, but at Nui [Mount] Do, in Thanh Hoa province, where the first vestiges of Lower Palaeolithic [Old Stone Age] were discovered, we have found traces of a Palaeolithic society dating back to between 300,000 and 500,000 years. [The earliest Palaeolithic Period dates back some 1,750,000 years, when prehistoric man emerged as a hunter and gatherer of vegetable food, using crude implements of carved bone and chipped stone.] The type of stone tools found at Nui Do corresponds to primitive industry dating back 500,000 years. Elsewhere, we have found vestiges of human activity corresponding to that of 300,000 years ago.

Pham Huy Thong explained that the enormous amount of earth-moving which went on during the war, had uncovered treasures of archaeological relics. Such excavations had uncovered layer after layer of evidence of the evolution of Vietnamese society. Even some of the huge craters gouged out by American bombs provided leads back to the past, duly noted by the dyke builders and repairers, and followed up by Pham Huy Thong and his teams of researchers. The pressing need for irrigation works in the immediate post-war period, to step up food production, entailed more earth-moving activities all over the country, and now it is almost a matter of course that, where earth is moved at sufficient depth along any of Vietnam's main rivers, it becomes an archaeologist's paradise.

To emphasize this point Professor Thong cited the example

of Yen Bai, in the province where the Hoa Binh Man was first discovered, where a big dam is now being built. Workers there led the archaeologists to vestiges of human habitation dating back 80,000 to 100,000 years. At Nghe An (the home province of Ho Chi Minh, in what for bombing purposes the US Air Force called the 'pan-handle' in the narrow waist of Central Vietnam) they found further irrefutable evidence of the Lower Palaeolithic Period, and at Son Vi (in the central regions of what used to be called the Bac Bo, or Tonking) they discovered relics of the Upper Palaeolithic Period, which specialists agree date back to between 20,000 and 8000 BC. These discoveries then clearly go back much further than the discoveries at Hoa Binh, which was first excavated in the late 1920s by the French archaeologist, Madeleine Colani. Her published work on the subject[1] created a sensation among archaeologists at the time. The discovery of a well-developed Stone Age culture in the natural caves and grottoes of Hoa Binh was the object of the First Congress of Far-East Pre-Historians, held in Hanoi in 1932. Archaeologists came flocking to Vietnam from all over the world. Among them was the American, Chester Gorman, who claimed to have discovered evidence of plant cultivation, which would have placed the Vietnamese amongst the world's earliest tillers of the soil. As far as rice cultivation is concerned, Professor Pham Huy Thong and other contemporary Vietnamese archaeologists believe they were the first rice growers, starting some thousand years before the Chinese. Modern methods of dating tools and rocks have produced new thinking on such matters, according to Professor Thong.

There are few authenticated ideas about primitive society. It was thought that agriculture had started in Mesopotamia from where it spread throughout the world, finally reaching China, Korea and South-East Asia. Now it is thought there were three great centres of agriculture. Mesopotamia, which grew wheat, Central America maize, and South-East Asia rice. Many of our specialists,

1. Madeleine Colani, *L'Age de la Pierre dans la Province de Hoa Binh, Memoires du Service Géologique de l'Indochine* (Hanoi, 1927).

based on the type of tools used, think that agriculture in South-East Asia started with Hoa Binh Man about 10,000 years ago and that, apart from rice, root crops were cultivated and a type of marrow. The melting of the world ice cap at the end of the last Glacial Age caused a big rise in the level of the sea [which some Western experts estimate at 400 feet] and a consequent shrinkage of the land surface in Asia. This caused man to interrupt his form of living and in South-East Asia – particularly affected by the land shrinkage – to turn to agriculture and domestication earlier than elsewhere. In any case, at Bac Son, we were able to trace the link between man the hunter, and man the cultivator and even livestock breeder. Among recent finds towards the terminal phase of our Neolithic Period – 6000 to 10,000 years ago – are vestiges of spinning and manufacture of fishing nets . . .

All this may seem very remote from the question of how the Vietnamese managed to throw successive invaders out of their territory and, even when they were defeated, to wage continuous armed struggle against the invaders. But if Pham Huy Thong and his colleagues are right – and they claim their evidence can stand up to the most rigorous scientific investigation – the fact that the roots of the Vietnamese people have been sunk into the same national soil since the dawn of mankind, could help explain the stubbornness with which they defend that soil. Generation after generation had added to the mastery of that soil, their irrigation works are amongst history's most ancient, with dykes and canals added to, century by century, year by year, until today. Not something lightly to be abandoned. It could explain why the northern frontier, despite incessant invasions by feudal China, has remained virtually intact throughout 2000 years. The southern frontier was expanded as feudal Vietnam did its part in expelling or absorbing other peoples – notably the Chams in Central Vietnam between the eleventh and seventeenth centuries and the Khmers (Cambodians) in the Mekong delta in the eighteenth century – until the Vietnamese occupied all the rice-growing lands of present-day Vietnam. The mountains which by and large formed the frontiers with Cambodia and Laos were occupied by ethnic groupings, mainly as part of a steady migratory process from China.

Until recently the origin of the Vietnamese nation was in the domain of myth and legend, perpetuated by word of mouth. The task of history-seekers was complicated by the fact that the Chinese invaders who annexed 'Nam Viet' as a province of China in 111 BC, in their zeal to force their own culture on the 'South Viets' as they called them, destroyed everything they could find in the way of cultural relics. This happened on subsequent occasions and was a constant practice of Chinese, Cham and Mongol invaders. Book-burning and the destruction of cultural symbols and, at a later stage, even the deportation of Vietnamese intellectuals to China, came under the heading of 'cultural assimilation'. This never succeeded, but an enormous amount of precious material, essential for Vietnamese scholars to piece their history together, was destroyed. As a result, often they have to turn to the famous Annals, which record the history of successive Chinese dynasties from 2225 to 247 BC, for scraps of information about their own country.

It should be noted that Vietnamese revolutionaries well understand that Chinese expansionism, like that of their own ancestors at the expense of the Chams and Khmers, was part of the normal nation-forming process of feudal states and not something to be held against today's Chinese, especially not on a racial basis. The support given by revolutionary China during the two twentieth-century wars – against the French and the Americans – emphasized in the most practical way the difference between revolutionary China and that of feudal, expansionist China.

Professor Pham Huy Thong noted that extensive evidence of clans and tribes dating back to the terminal Neolithic Period had been unearthed, especially around sites suitable for cultivation or fishing. Although the clans lived apart, it was clear that there were inter-clan relations. Relics of settlements, belonging to a later stage of development, some of which housed up to a thousand people – presumably multi-clan tribes – have also been found.

9

One of the most popular historical legends has it that Lac Long Quang, a lord of one of the fifteen tribes which had emerged at about 2000 BC in what is today northern Vietnam and which the Chinese called Viet Lac, married a beautiful creature called Au Co. Among their children were a hundred sons. One day, on what in modern divorce courts would be called grounds of 'incompatibility', they separated. 'I am a Dragon, you are a Fairy', legend has him saying. 'We can no longer remain together.' Fifty of the sons he took with him to the delta and coastal regions where he established a kingdom, the other fifty went with Au Co to the mountains. One of the sons who followed Long Quang inherited the throne and founded the Hung dynasty of eighteen successive rulers.[2] The account, drawn from the source noted, continues:

Legendary history puts the beginning of the Hung dynasty as far back as 4000 years ago. The 'kingdom' was called Van Lang and was made up of fifteen tribes, the main one being that of Me Linh, in Bach Hac, near present-day Viet Tri [on the Red river about 50 kms north-west of Hanoi]. The Hung kings ruled through *lac hau*, civilian chiefs; *lac tuong*, military chiefs; and *bo chinh*, subordinate officials. The throne was hereditary, so were probably the functions of *lac hau* and *lac tuong*. Thus an aristocracy had come into being, while primitive communes still subsisted, where social differentiation gradually deepened. Wars between various groups supplied slaves.

History again yields to the legend that the last of the Hung kings had a beautiful daughter who was courted by Son Tinh, the genie of the mountains, and Thuy Tinh, the water genie. The father ruled that whoever first arrived with the stipulated wedding gifts would get the bride. Son Tinh won and took her off to the mountains. The frustrated Thuy Tinh unleashed the waters against his rival but the latter stood firm. The battle

2. This is a slightly rephrased account of that which appears in *Vietnam: A Historical Sketch* (Hanoi, 1974). It was compiled by a team of scholars under the direction and editorship of the authoritative, French-trained historian Dr Nguyen Khac Vien.

10

is repeated every year since, with Son Tinh always winning. This legend could reflect the constant struggle against the floods caused almost every year by the rivers in spate at the time of the summer monsoon. It seems certain that right from the dawn of their history, the Vietnamese people had to organize themselves to bring the waters under control which implies some form of centralized organization, gradually consolidated as the deltas of the great rivers were conquered.

Thus it can be said if archaeology and related sciences provide reasons why the Vietnamese are stubborn in defence of their soil, legend touches on one of the keys to their unyielding, tenacious courage which has baffled and frustrated so many would-be conquerors.

When, after the victory over the United States and the Saigon régime, I asked Prime Minister Pham Van Dong how he explained the tenacity and stubborn quality of his people, he replied:

We don't get flustered. We have a marvellous nervous system, remaining calm and confident because throughout the centuries we have been forced into a perpetual struggle with nature and invaders. Our history is just that – struggle against nature and invaders. This is especially so in the North. In the South nature is more generous and the invaders have been less. The people there reflect that – they are more frank and spontaneous. In the North the daily, unending struggle formed tougher characters in every way. But our women, even the children, faced this latest terrible trial with confidence, with tenacity and serenity, because they knew that whether it was battle against floods, typhoons, droughts or foreign invaders, we always won.

Vietnamese historians are on solid ground from the third century BC onwards. The last of the Hung kings was defeated by the renowned An Duong, who ended a division into two tribal territories of what was then approximately North Vietnam of recent times, excepting the Central Highlands. In 258 BC, An Duong fused the principalities of Tay Au and Lac Viet to found the kingdom of Au Lac, setting up his

11

capital at Co Loa, only about 20 kms from today's Hanoi. Substantial ruins of the formidable star-shaped citadel he built at Co Loa exist to this day, a monument to Vietnamese antiquity and considerable skill in military engineering. Continuing research there has thrown much light on the state of Vietnamese civilization at the time. With some notable exceptions however, French historians and archaeologists, who started arriving at the beginning of this century, did not appear to be interested in helping the Vietnamese to discover their past. This is a point made by the French historian, Jean Chesneaux, one of the world's foremost specialists on Indochina.

'During the whole colonial period,' he wrote, 'and even since 1945, French scholars specializing in the study of the peoples of Indochina, their language, their history, their civilization, were financially and politically linked with the colonial authority. How could one expect of them any serious study of the Vietnamese nation, when the permanent negation of this reality in theory and in practice was the essential condition of maintaining that colonial authority? At most some studies – quite valuable in fact – could be undertaken in the fields of art or archaeology . . . But not a single study was made, for instance, of the peasant revolts in ancient Vietnam . . .'[3]

The very existence of a long line of Hung kings was poohpoohed and as Vietnamese scholars only had legends to justify the hypothesis they had no leg to stand on. In fact, there were discoveries of world historic importance to be made, but when someone stumbled across them, it appeared strenuous efforts were made to prove that they could not be attributed to the Vietnamese. Thus, it could be said that the French carried out the same type of cultural repression as had the Chinese. A good example of this attitude is the case of the Dong Son Civilization. In the early 1900s, a French customs' inspector looking for contraband along the coast of Thanh Hoa – about 150 kms due south of Hanoi – stumbled across a tomb with some bronze and iron implements inside.

3. Jean Chesneaux, *Contribution à l'Histoire de la Nation Vietnamienne* (Paris, 1955).

Experts headed for the spot. Excavation – and pillage – started, and the Dong Son bronzes were another 'world event', comparable to the discovery of the Hoa Binh Man. Archaeologists from half a dozen countries came, dug and left to publish their hypotheses, but they unanimously agreed that the bronzes could not be of Vietnamese origin. This was a point of contention made with some understandable energy by Professor Pham Huy Thong, who points out that the handling of the Dong Son discoveries was by no means the only attempt to exclude Vietnam from its own civilization. He claims, for example, that there is irrefutable evidence of the Hung kings, and all the signs are that the Metal Age dates back to their reign. And to return to Dong Son objects, he points out that archaeologists have found ones of similar type all along the basin of the Red river valley and, in addition, uncovered relics still older than Dong Son. He feels that this is proof indeed that the Dong Son metal-working industry was developed on the spot. More recent discoveries at Phung Nguyen – also in Thanh Hoa province close to Dong Son – indicate that the transition from Neolithic industry to the Metal Age took place about 4000 years ago.

Among the historical and archaeological proof of the existence of the Hung kings, from between 5000 and 4000 years ago, was the discovery of tombs of a number of them, the metal objects inside giving the clue to their age. Using radio-carbon C 14 the Vietnamese have dated the bronze and iron with reasonable accuracy. It seems clear from their findings that at first there were inter-tribal links which later grew into a confederation of tribal chiefs that subsequently gave rise to the kings. This system persisted between the eighth and third centuries BC, and corresponds to the legend of the eighteen dynasties. It also appears probable that after about 2000 BC, during which time the Neolithic industry remained static, there was a sudden leap forward in the eighth century BC and a consequent flourishing of culture in the terminal period.

The bronze drums, first discovered at Dong Son, but subsequently at fourteen other widely separated areas along the Red and Black rivers and in the Red river delta, date back 4000 years, but with decorations less evolved than those of 3000 years ago, which were the result of very high technique. Thus Professor Thong concludes that bronze was used by his ancestors from 4000 years ago, iron from 2500 years. Egypt, by comparison, had bronze drums of a quality similar to the Vietnamese 5000 years ago, and in China they appeared 3000 years ago. However, during the various Chinese invasions, there was a systematic destruction of the Vietnamese bronzes.

In the decorative engravings on the surface and walls of the drums, there is much to learn of the Vietnamese way of life 3000 to 4000 years ago. Almost all of those displayed in Hanoi's national museum, although dating from different periods and found in widely separated places, have a multi-rayed sun centred on the surface, surrounded by decorative elements of people at work and recreation, images of their houses on piles – similar to those in Cambodia today – men dressed as birds, probably the fabled *lac*, at fêtes or pounding rice. Big sea-going junks are portrayed. Much of the decoration is of geometric form with spirals and zig-zag patterns according to the fantasy of the artists and artisans.

The Co Loa citadel proved to be a treasure-trove of Bronze Age objects and it is surprising that French archaeologists, with such a potential nest-egg within fifteen minutes' drive of Hanoi, should have ignored it. It was, after all, almost 2500 years old, with an 8 km-long surrounding wall, 3 m to 4 m high with 12 m-wide ramparts. But it was in 1959, four years after the departure of the last of French occupation troops, that Vietnamese archaeologists found a stock of thousands of bronze arrowheads, together with bronze and stone battle-axes, and, in 1966, when American bombing of the Red river dykes required excavation works in the area, three bronze ploughshares were among the objects found.

Legend has it that as 'evil spirits' hampered the work of building the citadel. The genie of the Golden Tortoise, who often made his appearance at critical moments in Vietnamese history, came to help and, among other things, offered King An Duong a magic claw which, mounted as a trigger on his crossbow, transformed it into a super-weapon. The more prosaic Professor Thong believes that the legend arose from

14

the efficacy of the bronze warheads stocked so plentifully in An Duong's stronghold. In many cases, in fact, legend preserved elements of history faithfully enough to put scientists on the right track. As Professor Thong expressed it: 'Legends have been confirmed by history. Archaeology has illustrated facts of history previously considered as legends. Modern science has confirmed most of our recent interpretations of archaeological discoveries.' And concluding this part of our discussion, he added: 'One thing is clear. The Vietnamese Man was born and developed here. He evolved here, neither immigrant nor emigrant; remaining to defend his territory and whatever cultural values he had accumulated.'

Evidence is available that by the time the Chinese showed an interest in expanding south into what is now Vietnam, towards the end of the first millennium BC, they found a strong and vigorous civilization, bent on rejecting assimilation and ready to defend both territory and an original way of life.

CHAPTER 2

A THOUSAND-YEAR NIGHT

Among the most popular legends dating back to antiquity and one on a par with that of Son Tinh and Thuy Tinh is that of the boy prodigy, Thanh Giong who, on learning that the country was in danger, rapidly grew into a giant and irresistible warrior, wiping out the enemy with iron bars and bamboo trunks. 'He was accompanied by working people, fishermen, small buffalo-boys who also fought the enemy with hoes, sticks, their bamboo toys,' writes Vo Nguyen Giap, the former history teacher who founded the Vietnam People's Army and developed into one of the world's foremost military strategists. 'This oral tradition . . . exalted the heroic struggle of our ancestors against foreign aggression . . . This transparent and highly symbolic oral legend illustrated the old saying: "the whole people fight against an aggressor" . . . It is the image of our people in a period preceding that of written history . . .'[1]

As to why there was no written history, there are a few terse lines in the Introduction to a three-volume study of Vietnamese literature,[2] noting that, 'despite ten centuries of domination and a policy of tenacious assimilation', the

---

1. This and other quotes from Vo Nguyen Giap in this chapter are taken from his book *Armement des Masses Révolutionnaires, Edification de l'Armée du Peuple* (Hanoi, 1974).
2. *Anthologie de la Littérature Vietnamienne* (Hanoi, 1972).

17

Vietnamese people won their independence in the end and safeguarded their original national culture. But, 'of the long periods prior to the tenth century AD, no written vestige remains . . .' Except in the Chinese Annals of the period!

In 141 BC, 'strong man' Hsiao Wu-ti took over as Emperor in China and started restoring order in what historians agree was a chaotic situation which threatened the very existence of the Han dynasty (202 BC to AD 221). After having chastised the Hsien-Pi nomad rebels in the north and put down the Hsiung-Nu nomads who were causing trouble in the northwest, he turned his attention to the south and, after dealing with some secessionist-minded remnants of the Ch'in dynasty which had preceded the Hans, his troops invaded Au Lac, establishing a Han occupation régime. It was the first time the Vietnamese had experienced the shock of a well-organized invasion force. Although they had long been repulsing small incursions across their frontiers, they were not ready, organizationally or in any other way, to stand up to a challenge of such size and weight.

Historian Vo Nguyen Giap, who obviously did some research in the Chinese Annals, gives the following picture:

In the third century BC the inhabitants of Au Lac, together with other Viet tribes [now referred to as the ethnic minorities inhabiting the mountainous areas along the borders with China, Laos and Cambodia] fought aggressor troops for decades on end, choosing as their generals the bravest of the brave, fighting at night, launching surprise attacks, wiping out hundreds of thousands of enemy troops to finally bring off victory.

The organization of a national army especially formed to fight foreign aggressors, appeared very early in our history. The army of King An Duong included infantry and a navy. The Co Loa citadel was their common base. This army had at its disposal a very efficient arm, a sort of *ballista* [a catapult-type weapon developed from the crossbow, a primitive predecessor of the 'Katyusha', or multiple rocket-launcher, developed by the Soviet Union over 2000 years later] which simultaneously hurled a

18

great number of arrows tipped with highly efficient bronze points which were manufactured in great quantities. We have found several thousand of them in the Co Loa sector. This testifies to the early emergence of military organization with a certain level of development. The appearance of the *ballista* and bronze-tipped arrows marked great progress in our military technique at this period. Was this the origin of the legend of the magic crossbow?

General Giap then refers in his book to the unhappy sequel of the crossbow legend in which, while King An Duong was tricked into dalliance with a court beauty, a rival replaced the magic claw with an ordinary trigger. In his next battle An Duong, who had not noted the change, was defeated and the way opened for the Han invaders. Giap comments. 'Even with a magic crossbow, if one has lost the support of the people and relaxes vigilance, one cannot avert the misfortune of losing one's country. An Duong was defeated . . . From then on our country fell under the domination of feudal foreigners. For ten centuries on end our people never ceased rising up to fight for their national liberation, for the reconquest of their independence.'

The most important of the early insurrections was that in AD 43 led by the two sisters, Trung Trac and Trung Nhi. They were the first of a long line of women military leaders, ending in recent times with Nguyen Thi Dinh (the peasant woman from Ben Tre province who, on 17 January 1960, started the armed struggle in South Vietnam against the Saigon régime which ended on 30 April 1975, by which time she had long been Deputy Commander-in-Chief of the National Liberation Front's armed forces). In three years of brilliantly led operations, the Trung sisters expelled the Chinese occupation forces from the whole of Vietnamese territory as it was at that time. In AD 43, however, the Han invaders returned in force and the Trung sisters were defeated.

In his study Giap lists ten more important insurrections before Khuc Thua Du finally threw the Chinese out in 905 and Ngo Quen crushingly defeated a come-back attempt in 938.

(This was during the Five Dynasties and Ten States Period in China, 907–960.)

The fourth in chronological order of the ten important revolts mentioned by Vo Nguyen Giap, was also led by a woman, Trieu Thi Trinh, more popularly referred to as 'Dame Trieu'. She led a widespread insurrection which started in her home province of Thanh Hoa, in AD 238, and appears to have been a monumental peasant woman to whom legend attributes breasts 'one metre long', probably in deference to her military prowess. In any case Thanh Hoa people till this day mention this detail with pride, and link 'Dame Trieu' with modern local heroines like Nguyen Thi Hang, who headed an anti-aircraft unit defending Thanh Hoa's vital Hamrong bridge over the Ma river, on which ninety-nine American planes had been expended before it was finally put out of action in the closing stages of the air war against the North. At twenty-three years of age, legend has it that 'Dame Trieu' confided to her brother: 'My wish is to ride the tempest, tame the waves, kill the sharks. I want to drive out the enemy and save our people. I will not resign myself to our usual women's lot, bowing our heads to become concubines.' History records that, with her brother, she raised a powerful guerilla army and drove the Chinese out of the country. It took six months for the occupiers to assemble sufficient forces to re-invade and crush the rebels, 'Dame Trieu' committing suicide when all was lost.

It is noteworthy that the revolt of Vietnamese women – not only expressed on the battlefield – against the double subjection to Confucian-dictated male supremacy and to the foreign occupier, places them amongst the foremost pioneers of the feminist movement. Their long and continuing struggle for sexual equality inspired some of the finest works of Vietnamese literature, in form and content extremely advanced–not only for the period in which they were written, but for our own times. For ten centuries the various aspects of women's revolt could only be handed down through folk-songs, such as:

> Let's leave loyalty to the King to our father,
> Filial piety to our mother,
> Keeping love for ourselves.

20

Thus it was that the sense of personal humiliation imposed by feudal, Confucian morality, which denied women any rights at all, was fused with the sense of national humiliation of living under foreign overlords. The result was that a burning hatred of injustice became an important part of the Vietnamese character. As Nguyen Dinh Thi, a leading contemporary Vietnamese writer, once told me in trying to explain an aspect of the Vietnamese character: 'Our people can stand anything that comes from nature: flood, drought, heavenly injustice that wipes out their crops. What they cannot stand is human injustice. Raise the banner against man's injustice to man and, as our history shows, you can quickly raise an army.'

Therefore it was no accident that the armed forces of Ly Bi, who in the seventh century had led the most important insurrection after that of 'Dame Trieu', according to Giap, were called 'the troops of the just cause', a term which was used for those of successive insurrections right through to the nineteenth century. Quoting from *The Chronicle of the Ly Dynasty* (1009–1225), compiled after the Vietnamese had won the right to set down their own version of history, Vo Nguyen Giap writes:

The insurrection of the Ly Bi in the middle of the seventh century was on a large scale in the sense that it was able to 'gather heroes together from different provinces' in a simultaneous uprising. Within three months the power of the occupiers collapsed. The 'troops of the just cause' led by Ly Bi rapidly seized the Thanh Long (Hanoi) citadel and blow-by-blow repulsed the two counter-offensives of the occupiers . . .

After this victory the state of Van Xuan and its army were founded. In the war to safeguard the country which followed Ly Bi's army was defeated. But [his follower] Trieu Quang Phuc reorganized the armed forces and, withdrawing to the base of Ba Trach applying a 'protracted war' strategy, he employed the tactics of small engagements, isolated combats, surprise attacks, night attacks – to wear down the enemy. Then, when the enemy started to encounter grave difficulties at home, Trieu Quang Phuc went over to the counter-offensive, defied the army of aggression and won back the country's independence. The independent state of Van Xuan lasted for over half a century. For that period it represented a great victory. The idea of protracted war was born. The skirmish, surprise attacks, night attacks – had all attained a new degree of development . . .

From Giap's admiration for these typical guerilla tactics one senses the influence they had on his own military thinking. With his studies as a historian, he read everything he could lay hands on regarding the developments of the arts of war of his ancestors, carefully noting strategies and tactics well tested throughout the centuries as suitable for Vietnamese conditions and temperament. It is in Giap's summary of twenty centuries of Vietnam's history that one finds the key to his own military thinking which later enabled him to outwit the most illustrious generals that France, and finally the United States, could field. The fact that the United States had only 200 years of experience on which to draw and Vietnam 2000 years, was probably one of the factors of the US withdrawal. And a major factor in the defeat of the Saigon régime and its American-trained generals was that its leaders turned their backs on the experiences of their ancestors and based their strategies and tactics on those of the United States.

Giap, whom Ho Chi Minh was to entrust with the task of organizing what was to develop into the Vietnam People's Army, studied the works of the world's classical military theorists, digesting everything he could find about the Soviet and Chinese experiences. But he developed a specifically Vietnamese type of People's War, deeply rooted in Vietnam's own military history. He learned much from those who finally wrested independence from the Chinese, and still more from those who defended that independence, especially those who threw back the Mongols in the thirteenth century, and the Ming and Ch'ing invaders in the fifteenth and eighteenth centuries respectively. And, although he deals with only the great highlights of Vietnam's military history, he notes – as

22

during the three centuries which followed the collapse of the Van Xuan state – that: 'The people never ceased to revolt, fighting the enemy arms in hand and launching numerous insurrections.' This was something that neither the French nor the Americans could ever understand. No sooner was one district or province declared secure than there was a flare-up in a neighbouring one, and while the fire was being put out there it broke out again in the 'pacified' one.

At the beginning of the tenth century, China was in one of those periods of chaos which always preceded the collapse of a dynasty. Plagued with peasant revolts and dissensions among warlord-type generals, the T'ang dynasty was running out of steam. In 905, the year before the collapse, the Chinese Proconsul in Vietnam, having started to practise some local warlordism, was downgraded and subsequently executed. A Vietnamese patriot, Khuc Thua Du, took over, named himself the new Proconsul and declared national independence. China, under the confused and short-lived Five Dynasties and Ten States, reacted as usual by sending in successive invasion forces to restore order.

In 938 there was a decisive battle on the majestic Bach Dang river, which runs intő the South China sea north of Haiphong, a major invasion route for Chinese and Mongols in their various incursions into Vietnam. A new leader, Ngo Quen, had emerged with a devastating new tactic against invasion fleets. The Bach Dang is tidal, being shallow at low tide. Ngo Quen had iron-tipped, pointed stakes firmly embedded into the bed of the main channel and lured the Chinese invasion convoy up the river at high tide when the tree-trunk stakes were invisible. At the turn of the tide, and when the whole convoy was well upstream, Ngo Quen's light combat junks engaged the much heavier Chinese vessels, forcing them to turn back. Inevitably caught in the stake traps, the Chinese fleet was an easy mark for the fire-arrows of Ngo Quen's archers. The invaders were wiped out almost to the last man, including their commander, General Huang-tao. Giap considers that the Bach Dang victory marked a great turning-point in Vietnamese history, and heralded an era in which his people achieved total independence, building up and developing a feudal state based on the whole people under arms and not dependent on mercenaries.

In a discussion on this point with historian Dr Nguyen Khac Vien, his view was that Vietnam was the first pre-capitalist state to decree universal military training and thus establish a permanent reserve of peasant soldiers – usually with their arms stocked in their home villages – on call in case of a foreign invasion. It was a system started in embryo form by Khuc Thua Du, taken over by the Ly dynasty when it was established in 1009, and developed by successive rulers as the various dynasties waxed and waned.

Following the expulsion of the Chinese there were half a dozen decades of fighting between feudal rivals before the Ly dynasty emerged. Its founder, Ly Thai To, promptly set up his capital in Thanh Long (Hanoi) and it was to remain there for the next 900 years until the early nineteenth century, pro-French, Nguyen dynasty founded and established its capital at Hue, in Central Vietnam. According to Nguyen Khac Vien, the first two decrees of Ly Thai To ordered a general amnesty for 'collaborators' with the Chinese and the destruction of all instruments of torture!

On the subject of compulsory military service during the Ly dynasty, Vo Nguyen Giap notes that following the setting up of the centralized feudal state, a census was introduced for recruitment purposes. Thus the armed forces were called upon to fight when required and returned to the countryside after the battle. Employing this system, with a limited but permanent nucleus, the feudal state of the day could mobilize ten army groups, totalling about a million men.

Giap then comes to a point crucial to his own organization of the armed forces of the Vietnamese revolution: the three-tier system later adopted by his counterparts in Laos and Cambodia, which was the secret of the even quality of their regular forces and the possibility of immediate replacement of battlefield losses with highly trained veterans. The Vietnamese People's Army was neither modelled on the armed forces of the Chinese revolution – although this must have been tempting – nor on those of the Soviet Union. It was formed from the accumulated experience of Vietnamese warriors fighting under conditions which would remain a constant throughout the country's history.

Based on the system of the 'whole people under arms', the feudal state built up three categories of troops. The Court troops at the central echelon; regional troops of the great lords, and tribal chiefs among the ethnic minorities; the *huong binh* and *dan binh* – the local troops at village and hamlet level. The Court troops were called 'Sons of Heaven', under the Dinh-Le [the transitional rulers who exercised power between Ngo Quen's defeat of the Chinese and the establishment of the Ly dynasty]; 'Permanent Troops' under the Ly, and 'Troops Under Arms' in the Tran dynasty (1225–1411). These were the troops on active service and what we today call the permanent army. As for the regional troops in the countryside who 'in times of peace returned to their homes to cultivate the ricefields and in case of alert could be called to the colours', they were called 'external forces', analogous to those whom today we would call 'reservists'. The *huong binh* and *dan binh* were used by the feudal administration in times of peace to maintain the domination of the feudal state in the hamlets and villages; in times of war they would fight against the aggressor on the side of the people, thus constituting a broad-based People's Army...

Here already in developed form was the pattern Giap was to adopt early in his military career, namely the regular army, set up to conduct operations anywhere on the national territory and to 'fulfil international obligations'; the regional forces, full-time armed units operating within specific geographic or administrative boundaries; and the self-defence guerillas, part-time soldiers, part-time peasants, charged essentially with the defence of their own hamlets and villages. As young men and women reached military age, they automatically enrolled in their local self-defence guerilla organization. From there they graduated – the young men at least – into the regional forces as necessity arose, and in the regional forces the regular army had an inexhaustible reserve of combat-hardened

25

reinforcements. Although each of the three had their own specific functions, their activities could be co-ordinated when occasion demanded. It was a system eminently suited to People's War because troops of one category or another, drawn from the people who supported them, were always in place, independent of transport and supplies. During the 1946–54 war against the French, each province – even in the occupied regions – was expected to maintain one battalion of regional troops, each district one company, each village one platoon of self-defence guerillas. In the war against the US-Saigon régime (1960–75), the number of units was much higher at provincial and district level. In Long An, the Mekong delta province closest to Saigon, there were always between four and six regional battalions. At village level there were less because of the US policy of 'urbanization', the forced evacuation of the countryside by massive bombings and chemical warfare.

The fullest expression of the advantages of the three-tier system was displayed during The 1975 Spring Offensive. But the system had proved itself from the beginnings of Vietnam as an independent state. Giap describes how it was employed to good effect by a mandarin eunuch whose real name was Ngo Tuan, but who so distinguished himself on the battlefield that he was co-opted into the Ly dynasty under the name of Ly Thuong Kiet. He enters Vietnam's history as one of its most illustrious generals, having repulsed the eleventh-century invasions by the Chams and those of the expeditionary force of the Chinese Sung dynasty (960–1279).

The Sung invasion took place in 1077, but the expeditionary corps never succeeded in crossing the Nhu Quyet river. Eventually, Ly Thuong Kiet, who proved himself as excellent a diplomat as a military strategist, brought about a peace settlement, saving Chinese face by ceding five frontier districts which he recovered two years later through negotiations. For almost two centuries Dai (Great) Viet – the name adopted by the Ly dynasty – enjoyed relative peace along its northern borders. The next great trial was in the mid thirteenth century when Kublai, grandson of world-conqueror Genghis Khan, turned his attention to Dai Viet. By that time the Ly dynasty had been replaced by that of the Tran.

CHAPTER 3

OF MONGOLS AND MINGS

Grandfather Genghis Khan could die peacefully in 1225, content that one of the last great campaigns – which he had personally directed – had brought his hordes to the gates of Peking, assuring an abundance of rich pasture lands for all imaginable horses and herds for 'ten thousand generations'. His horsemen warriors had overrun the vast rolling grasslands of Manchuria, stretching from Mongolia's front door to the Sea of Japan and the East China sea. Grandson Kublai who, after some serious family squabbles, assumed the succession, was not, however, satisfied to leave things as he inherited them, even though by then the Empire included a goodly part of northern China. With that obsession for expansion of all those who inherited the hot blood of Genghis, his eyes turned east towards Korea and Japan and south to the rest of China and to the kingdoms of Dai Viet and Champa still further south.

The Yellow and Yangtze rivers were tough nuts for armies of horsemen to crack, so Kublai Khan conceived the idea of first occupying China's south-west provinces of Szechuan and Yunnan, then outflanking the great rivers south of Peking by pushing across through Dai Viet and entering China from the south. Having taken four years to digest Yunnan province, occupied in 1253, Kublai's generals demanded passage

27

through Dai Viet, but the Tran rulers refused. So the Mongols tried to secure by force of arms what they had been refused by diplomacy. In a brief campaign launched in 1257, which resulted in the Mongols sacking the largely deserted capital of Thanh Long, then running into a 'scorched earth' country-side, an abundance of tropical disease and harassment from all sides by *dan binh* guerillas, Kublai's troops started to withdraw. In doing so they suffered heavy losses from attacks by the Muong and other ethnic minorities as they tried to make their way back to Yunnan through the thick jungles bordering the Red river. This was obviously not the sort of thing that a man of Kublai Khan's status and lineage would take lying down. But the victory gave the Trans a good thirty years' respite, while Kublai gobbled up the rest of China by more direct means, consolidating his empire with Peking as its capital. During this time the Trans had a not too irksome vassal-type arrangement with Peking, which involved paying annual tribute only.

Towards the end of the 1270s, however, there were signs that the Mongols were preparing to move south again with Dai Viet and Champa the main objectives. Kublai Khan, who all accounts agree was an astute politician, tried to take Dai Viet the 'soft way'. In 1281, he persuaded Tran Di Ai, a scion of the Tran dynasty on a diplomatic mission to Peking, to return with a Mongol escort as a puppet king of Dai Viet. The scheme failed. Tran Dai Ai was arrested as soon as he crossed the frontier, and the Mongol escort were lucky to get back alive. The Dai Viet leadership had no illusions as to what was coming.

The following year, the Mongols bypassed Dai Viet and invaded Champa by a sea-borne expedition, putting the capital to the 'fire and sword' in traditional Mongol style. In the face of fierce Cham resistance, however, they gradually with-drew their forces and massed them along the Champa–Dai Viet border. This was accompanied by the massing of very large Mongol forces along the China–Dai Viet border, to-gether with a demand that they be granted transit rights through Dai Viet to attack the Chams in the south. The re-quest was refused – the second time the Dai Viet rulers had denied their territory for the Mongols to attack a third country.[1]

That not all the ancestors felt that way is clear from the impassioned appeal to his fellow officers by Tran Quoc Tuan, better known to historians as General Tran Hung Dao, the famous strategist who defeated the Mongols. The appeal, considered by Vietnamese as one of the early gems of their literature, was written at a moment when 500,000 Mongol horsemen and foot soldiers were massed on the Chinese–Dai Viet frontier, either to link up with the remnants of the Champa invasion pushing north, or to invest Dai Viet and push on south to occupy the whole Indochinese peninsula. While King Tran Nhan Ton was keenly aware of the dramatic situation, his kinsman, Tran Hung Dao, felt there was far too much wining, dining and dalliance going on in Court circles at a moment when the whole nation should have been on its tiptoes. Recalling the heroes and patriots of the past who had shrunk from no sacrifices to expel foreign invaders, Tran Hung Dao spoke bitterly in his Appeal of the insolence and arrogance of the Mongol envoys in the Dai Viet capital, castigating the indifference of his brother officers to such humiliations.

He exhorted his officers to pull themselves together; to train their soldiers properly, especially in bowmanship, so that each man, each family 'should be the equal of a Bang Mong and Hau Nghe' (mythical Chinese archers). It was in this impassioned Appeal that Tran Hung Dao revealed that he had prepared a book, *Summary of Military Strategy*, which 'represents a synthesis of the writings of the great strategists of all times', as he expressed it, advising his officers to study it carefully. Generals Vo Nguyen Giap and Van Tien Dung highly valued Tran Hung Dao's military text-book. Other Vietnamese military scientists have compared it with the

1. When some 700 years later, I asked Ngo Dien, the Assistant Foreign Minister in Charge of Information of the Socialist Republic of Vietnam, whether these two refusals were not an early manifestation of Vietnam's leaning towards what is now the official policy of 'non-alignment', he grinned and said: 'No. The records show that our ancestors were simply convinced that "transit rights" would turn into permanent occupation. What it does show is that our ancestors, as always, were very determined to defend national independence.'

works of Sun Tzu (the Chinese general who, in 500 BC, set forth the basic principles of how to win battles and wars) and of Clausewitz, the nineteenth-century German military theoretician.

Whether it was the result of Tran Hung Dao's Appeal or not, Vietnamese historians record that when King Tran Nhan Ton convened an assembly of princes and high dignitaries who comprised the top military hierarchy, to inform them of the impending Mongol invasion and put the question: 'Do we fight, or do we capitulate?', the reply was a thunderous: 'We fight.' He then called a second assembly of village chiefs from all over the country. Same question, same unhesitating answer. The King then advised the village chiefs: 'If you see the Mongols coming, hide your rice and yourselves in the forest.'

At the end of 1284, the huge Mongol army under Kublai Khan's son, General Toghan, crossed into Dai Viet from the north and a few months later those massed on the Champa–Dai Viet frontier started moving up from the south, under General Toa Do. The Trans had an estimated 200,000 troops, about 20,000 of which were of the regular army.

In the early stages of the invasion the Vietnamese could play little more than a harassing role. Toghan's forces gradually pushed south, crossing the Red river early in 1285 to capture Thanh Long. On Tran Hung Dao's advice, the capital had been evacuated but the Mongols, as was their habit, burned the capital and massacred any of the population who had remained. After attempts to win over one of the captured Tran generals – Tran Binh Trong – failed, he was executed. Vietnamese forces under Tran Quang Khai which tried to block the forces advancing from the south were badly beaten in Nghe An province. Within a few months of the invasion therefore, the Mongols were masters of the greater part of the Red river delta and of Thanh Hoa and Nghe An provinces – in fact the greater part of the country.

However, the Vietnamese were constantly harassing the widely scattered Mongol troops and, when Toa Do's troops, plagued by guerillas, tried to move up towards the Red river and join the Mongol army stationed further north, the Tran

30

sent 50,000 men to meet them. As a result, the Mongols suffered a severe defeat at Ham Tu (in Tran Hung Dao's home province of Hai Hung), a defeat which began to sound the retreat for the Mongol forces. By August 1285, the whole country was liberated and the Mongol army of half a million men beaten. Toghan, referred to by the Vietnamese as Thoat Hoan, escaped into China by hiding in a bronze cask.

It was at this point that Kublai Khan had to cancel his plans for a third attempted invasion of Japan, in order to prepare a third attack on the Dai Viet. (Two previous attempts against Japan, in 1274 and 1281, had been thwarted, mainly by the intervention of the *kamikazi* (Divine Wind) which wrecked most of the invasion fleets.) It is interesting to note that in defeating the second Mongol invasion Tran Hung Dao was applying what was later to become one of Vo Nguyen Giap's unbeatable strategies of catching the enemy in the fatal contradiction of dispersal or concentration of his troops. Dispersal to hold territory, concentration for launching strong attacks. Sacrifice dispersal and you lose territory; sacrifice concentration, you are likely to find yourself outnumbered in key areas. Giap time and again, in the two resistance wars, forced his adversaries into this dilemma. If they dispersed he forced them to concentrate; if they chose concentration he forced them to disperse, always maintaining the strategic initiative, keeping the enemy off balance. The other strategy that Tran Hung Dao applied was later to be formulated by Mao Tse-tung. 'When the enemy attacks, withdraw. When the enemy tires, harass. When the enemy retreats, attack.'

Kublai and his son lost no time in trying to avenge the defeat. With Toghan again commander-in-chief and Omar his second-in-command, an army of 300,000 under Toghan invaded from the north at the end of 1287, while a huge invasion fleet commanded by Omar headed south for the Bach Dang river. Again, what was left of the capital was evacuated; again the Mongols seized it, burning whatever had been rebuilt; but again they experienced a barren land and a population which evaporated as they advanced. A main sea-borne supply convoy was captured almost intact in Ha Long Bay (one of the world's greatest and most beautiful natural har-

31

bours) as it was heading for the Bach Dang river. The convoy
fleet was destroyed and all supplies seized. This together with
the scorched-earth policy was a major disaster and Toghan's
generals started to mutter about retreat. A still worse catas-
trophe was to come, however.

Ngo Quen's old stratagem was repeated to deal with Omar's
invasion fleet sailing up the Bach Dang river. Iron-tipped stakes
were driven into the river bed. A small Vietnamese fleet
lured Omar's junks upstream to a point where Tran Hung
Dao's main force was in position to attack them just after
the tide had started to turn. In a confused manoeuvre, Omar's
fleet turned round to make for the wider waters of the Bach
Dang estuary, but got caught up in the labyrinth of stakes, an
easy prey for Tran Hung Dao's archers with their fire-arrows.
In one of the most complete victories in Vietnamese history,
the entire Mongol fleet was destroyed – 100 junks burned or
sunk, the other 400 captured together with Admiral Omar.

On learning of this disaster, Toghan started to withdraw,
but during the retreat his troops were decimated by those of
Tran Hung Dao's son-in-law, General Pham Ngu Lao, who
had been sent to occupy the Lang Son mountain passes and
inflict maximum damage on the Mongols retreating into
China. This then was the third Mongol defeat. When Kublai
died in 1294, his son Timur discarded plans for a further invasion, electing to establish friendly relations with the Dai
Viet, which continued to pay yearly tribute to the Mongol
Court, upholding an agreement made six years previously.

Vo Nguyen Giap has always admired the political approach
to warfare shown by Tran Hung Dao and his capacity to
mobilize the masses of the people. His victories were possible,
Giap concluded, because 'the whole country united its forces
to drive out the invaders'.[2] The study of the three Mongol
campaigns certainly influenced Giap in his own concepts of
'People's War' and in the importance of not trying to defend
'prestige' positions, even if they included the country's capital.
It was thus that in 1946, the new-born Vietnam People's Army
did not defend Hanoi to the last, but fought a delaying action

2. *Armement des Masses Révolutionnaires, Edification de l'Armée du Peuple*,
op cit, p 68.

32

to make the French pay heavily for its capture. They thus gained time to evacuate important equipment from the capital to enable the waging of protracted war from the jungle.

King Tran Nhon Ton, having presided over two of the three resounding victories over the Mongols and ushered in an era of peace, retired to a Buddhist monastery in 1293; Tran Hung Dao died in 1300, and shortly after this the Tran dynasty entered a period of decline. If the peasantry throughout Vietnamese history always resisted invaders and supported the feudal dynastic rulers when they did the same, it was also true that when no foreign invasion was threatened the peasantry had its usual antagonistic relations with the feudal landowners. Such a class had started to emerge, especially at the start of the Tran dynasty. More and more of the nobles and mandarins, exploiting their status in the feudal hierarchy, encroached upon what had been communal lands or even those of small proprietors. The process was kept in check during the reign of the early Trans but, by the mid fourteenth century, there were numerous peasant insurrections which gradually led to a serious weakening of the Tran dynasty. At the end of the century a usurper, Ho Quy Ly, seized the throne, proclaiming himself the founder of a Ho dynasty. In China the Mongol dynasty had also gone into a decline following the defeats in Vietnam and the death of Kublai Khan. It was the turn of the Mings (1368–1644) to provide a period of rule in China between the Mongols and the Ch'ings (Manchus). On the pretext of wanting to help put the Trans back in power, a Ming army invaded Vietnam in 1407, quickly defeating Ho Quy Ly who based himself exclusively on the Court army and not on the people's forces. In an attempt to defend fixed positions he was easily beaten. Some of the Tran princes tried to take advantage of difficulties the Ming were having at home with Mongol remnants, to stage a comeback. But they were divided among themselves, had lost popular support and were easily defeated, all their leaders being captured.

For twenty years, then, from 1407 to 1427, Dai Viet was incorporated again as a province of the Chinese Empire, and ruled directly from Peking. The country was divided up into administrative regions according to the Chinese pattern and

33

assimilation was attempted on an unprecedented scale.

As the princes and aristocrats had failed to defend the nation, it was left to a commoner to take the lead, Le Loi, a small landowner from Thanh Hao province where so much of Vietnam's history has originated. He had as his political adviser one of the most remarkable figures of Vietnamese history, Nguyen Trai, poet, philosopher, statesman and outstanding military strategist.

It is no accident that in revolutionary Vietnam there are always two officers listed as commanding armies, divisions and so on all the way down the line, the military and the political commander each having their clearly defined functions. Thus it was on 7 February 1418 that landowner Le Loi, in the name of about 1000 followers, proclaimed himself king, taking the name of Binh Dinh Vuong, inviting all who opposed the Ming domination to rally to his banner. As will be noted later, audacity has always been a key and successful weapon in the Vietnamese armoury.

For the next five years, with the usual ups and downs associated with guerilla warfare, Le Loi and Nguyen Trai fought it out with the Ming troops in Thanh Hoa province. In 1423, the Ming command asked for a truce during which an unsuccessful attempt was made to buy off Le Loi. The truce gave him time to consolidate his position, to build up new bases in neighbouring Nghe An province and gradually to capitalize on peasant support to expand his control over the whole country south of the Red river, except for a few isolated citadels. In 1426, the Ming sent in 50,000 reinforcing troops with a famous general, Vuong Thong (a Vietnamization presumably of Wang Tong), in overall command. In two main columns, they advanced along the widely separated traditional invasion routes from Yunnan in the north-west and through the Lang Son pass in the north-east. Le Loi went over to the counter-offensive sending two armies to intercept each of the enemy columns and a third directly against Thanh Long. The outcome of all this was that Vuong Thong's troops were forced to fight their way through successive encirclements, the survivors joining up with other Ming troops in the Thanh Long citadel, where they were promptly besieged.

Nguyen Trai then engaged in a psychological warfare exercise which Vo Nguyen Giap added to his military arsenal by the creation of special units trained in the art of persuading enemy troops that it was in their best interests to lay down their weapons and return to their villages. 'Better conquer hearts than citadels', Nguyen Trai had written in a letter offering his services to Le Loi. He set the example by an exchange of letters – his, full of irony – with Vuong Thong, the besieged Ming generalissimo. These letters are considered to be treasures of Vietnamese literature. In one letter, Nguyen Trai was prepared to give safe passage to Vuong Thong's troops, but Vuong Thong's reply, which was that he had no powers to negotiate a settlement, was received with scepticism by Nguyen Trai. Indeed, it was clear that the besieged general was playing for time for more reinforcements to arrive from China. Nguyen Trai knew this, but he was also genuinely interested in saving lives, those of his own men as well as those of the Mings. However, after several more exchanges, and little or no progress, except that Nguyen Trai had received proof that reinforcements were on the way, the Vietnamese patience was apparently growing thin. Le Loi and his troops were particularly anxious to join battle, so Nguyen Trai exhorted Vuong Thong to avoid the inevitable massacre that would take place if the citadel had to be taken by storm. He also went to an extreme length in further pledges to respect traditional links with China:

Our two countries can renew their links of friendship, the war will end for all time. If you want to withdraw your troops the roads, as well as the junks, are ready. By road or by sea – the choice is yours in complete security. I will be satisfied with my rank of vassal and will pay the customary tribute. If you want it otherwise, dispose your troops in battle formation so that our armies confront each other once and for all in open fields to see who wins the day. But stop burying yourself away like an old invalid.'[3]

3. *Anthologie de la Littérature Vietnamienne*, Vol 1, op cit, pp 161–2.

It was not the first time nor the last – as probably Henry Kissinger remembers – that foreigners took Vietnamese generosity for weakness, apparently missing the chance for terms of settlement which would be better than those available in three months' time, and infinitely better than those they could have in three years' time. In the Nguyen Trai–Vuong Thong exchange of letters, curiously similar to the Kissinger–Le Duc Tho secret talks in Paris in 1971, Nguyen Trai was offering – as did Le Duc Tho – the face-saving solution. When it was turned down, not once, twice or thrice, but a dozen times, Nguyen Trai reluctantly had to don battledress, just, as will be noted, Le Duc Tho left the Paris diplomatic arena to don his battledress and help direct the final military campaign that crushed US hopes in South Vietnam. Vuong Thong must have believed that his delaying tactics had won the day when he received the news that in October 1427 further strong Ming reinforcements were on the way. One hundred thousand troops came through the Lang Son pass and another 50,000 from Yunnan down the Red river valley.

What happened then is described in a remarkable piece of war reporting by Nguyen Trai, known as a Proclamation of Victory, presented in the form of an epic poem. It starts with a statement of principle as to the war aims:

> Peace and happiness for the people – these are the basis for humanity and justice.

> Eliminate violence, the primary role assigned to our combatants.

Giving the background of oppressions which forced Le Loi to take to arms, Nguyen Trai describes the loneliness and trials of their small band during the first years in the jungle:

> Living on gall, sleeping on thorns,
> Scanning the past, gauging the future, weighing the chances of victory.

Gradually the people flocked to their banners and Le Loi's

forces were able to carry out harassing attacks, ambushes, hitting the enemy where he least expected:

> In a thousand ambushes we wiped out big armies with
>   small forces.
> The just cause triumphed over barbarism.
> Man vanquished brute force.
> At Bo Dang we struck like a thunderbolt,
> At Tra Lan we split enemy armies like bamboo.

Through numerous defeats, great and small, the Chinese forces were obliged to withdraw into fortresses and citadels, where they were closely surrounded. This was the basis for the exchange of letters between Nguyen Trai and the Chinese Commander-in-Chief, Vuong Thong, offering safe passage for a Chinese withdrawal. When this was refused and Chinese reinforcements started to pour across the border in two large columns, from the north over the Lang Son passes and the west from Yunnan, Le Loi went over to the offensive, as Nguyen Trai describes:

> The ninth month of the year, Lieu Thang crossed the Lang
>   Son pass,
> The tenth month, Moc Thanh, from Yunnan,
> Advanced their armies.
> We wiped out their advance units, cut their road of re-
>   treat, their supply lines,
> The 18th at Chi Lang – Lieu Thang was beaten,
> The 20th beaten again at Ma An, he lost his life.
> The 25th, Count Luong Minh perished in the heat of
>   battle,
> The 28th, confronted with defeat, minister Ly Khanh
>   took his life.
> Pressing our advantage we continued the advance . . .

Having dealt with the reinforcements and occupied all the roads of retreat, Le Loi then attacked the encircled garrisons, and the main battle started. Many of the enemy garrisons, seeing their situation was hopeless, killed their officers and

37

surrendered. They were particularly terrified by Le Loi's use of elephants which had received meticulous military training and were used to spearhead the advance like tanks in modern armies:

> When our elephants drank, streams dried up.
> At the first thunder of our drums, sharks and crocodiles fled,
> At the second not even a bird was left.
> We are the hurricane that sweeps away dried leaves,
> The ants that make even dyke walls collapse.
> On his knees, general Thoi Tu begs mercy,
> Binding his hands minister Hoang Phuc surrenders,
> The roads of Lang Giang, of Lang Son, are choked with enemy dead.
> At Xuong Giang and Binh Than, the rivers are crimson with blood,
> Winds and clouds have changed colour, sun and moon have paled.

As with that inflicted on the Mongols, Le Loi's victory was total, but as throughout most of their history, the Vietnamese were generous at the moment of victory, perhaps part of the wisdom required for the survival of a small people always battling with more powerful ones. This is implicit in the final stanzas of Nguyen Trai's Proclamation – issued in the name of Le Loi:

> Their captured generals, impotent tigers, beg for forgiveness.
> We have fought not to sow death,
> By the will of heaven we have opened to them the way of life.
> To Ma Ky, to Phuong Chinh, we gave five hundred junks.
> To Vuong Thong and Ma Anh, thousands of horses to return home.
> On the high seas they were still green with fear,
> Until they reached home they still trembled with fright,
> Dreading death, they pleaded for peace,

38

As for us we wanted peace and quiet for all,
This was our wisdom.
The Motherland is safe and sound,
Our mountains and rivers will grow new skins,
Peace follows war, day the night . . .
The four seas are calm for all time; everywhere blows the
    wind of renewal.
Let this be known far and wide![4]

The entire Proclamation notably exalts the spirit of patriotism, national unity and humanism; the concept of clemency in sending prisoners immediately back to their homes. And, despite the historic victory, there is no glorification of militarism. Indeed, like the letters to Vuong Thong, it is permeated with the spirit of going to extreme lengths to avoid bloodshed, but once this was inevitable, the intention to get it over as quickly as possible at minimum cost and return to cultivating the arts of peace was of prime importance. Nguyen Trai was a prodigious worker. Apart from the Proclamation and his manual on the art of war, he prepared one of the first geographies of the Vietnam of his day; a history of the Le Loi uprising; a large collection of poems in classical Chinese; and 254 poems in *nom*. The use of *nom* represented a key weapon in resisting Chinese cultural assimilation and was typical of the Vietnamese genius in extracting 'good from evil'. The Chinese tried to impose their language and stamp out Vietnamese. The Vietnamese accepted written Chinese but used the ideographs to express their own language. In other words, in *nom* the ideographs meant the same thing to the Chinese and Vietnamese, but the spoken word remained Vietnamese and thus the language was preserved. Nguyen Trai's poems were the first important literary works to be written in *nom*.

The Proclamation remained a classic work, which grew in popularity as the centuries passed, and is another of those factors which passed into the national bloodstream to produce that serenity and confidence in final victory under even the

4. Extracts taken from *Anthologie de la Littérature Vietnamienne*, Vol 1, op cit, pp 143–8.

most impossible circumstances. Unfortunately Nguyen Trai's prediction of peace for 'ten thousand generations' was not fulfilled, but at least the Mings never tried again.

Due to Court intrigues, Nguyen Trai later withdrew from public life and retired to his lovely residence, surrounded by a wood of pine and bamboo through which meandered a tinkling stream, in what is now Hai Hung province, a few kms from the native village of Tran Hung Dao, about 70 kms north-east of Hanoi, not far from the Bach Dang river. Turning his back on Court intrigues, and rivals jealous of his prestige and influence, he spent his days writing poetry and playing chess. Le Loi was already dead and Nguyen Trai's Court enemies took advantage of the death of his successor, the young king Le That Thong, to accuse the great scholar-patriot of being involved in regicide. Nguyen Trai and his whole family were put to death in 1428, but were posthumously rehabilitated by That Thong's son, King Le Thanh Tong, some twenty years later.

By all standards of all ages and countries, Nguyen Trai was a very great man, one who has exerted a strong and positive influence on the Vietnamese character until today.

CHAPTER 4

CONTINUITY

That Vo Nguyen Giap would take to heart
the new lessons to be learned from the genius of Nguyen Trai
and the defeat of the Mings was natural, and the points he
stresses in all his writings give a clue to much of his thinking,
above all, his passion for People's War and conviction that
even with modern weaponry, classical warfare must always be
combined with People's War.

Shortly after the first US combat troops were disembarked
at Danang, in March 1965,[1] and the American press began
speculating that this was the beginning of a build-up to invade
the North, I asked Ho Chi Minh what he thought. 'Of course,
we take the possibility very much into consideration,' he
said, 'but it reminds me of a fox that has one foot caught in a
trap. He starts leaping about to try to get out and, pouf, he
lands a second foot in a trap. That will happen if the Americans
are mad enough to invade the North. But you had better

---

1. In the first days of 1965, élite Saigon forces suffered a shattering defeat
at the battle of Binh Gia, followed by several more in the weeks that followed.
This started a grave political crisis in Saigon, leading to the fall of successive
governments, and there were prospects of a complete collapse. To stiffen morale,
the United States started bombing North Vietnam in February 1965, following
this up by sending the Marines into Danang without, as it transpired later,
any formal request from the Saigon Government. This marked the start of
direct US combat involvement in the Vietnam war.

41

speak to Giap about it.' Giap was his usual serene self, with his gently ironic smile as I quoted from some American press reports, sceptical about North Vietnamese 'outmoded' military equipment which they assumed was still that captured from the French at Dien Bien Phu in 1954 and of a Vo Nguyen Giap still living in the days of People's War. The implication was that a push to the North would be a 'walkover' and the American people had nothing to worry about.

'Let them try', said Giap. 'We would welcome them to come where we can get them with modern weapons which our comrades in the South don't have. Wherever they can usefully disembark will be within range of our heavy weapons. But they will also find themselves caught up in People's War. The whole people are united as they were under our ancestors and they will find every village a hornets' nest. Whenever and wherever we fight it will always be People's War!' It was more than ever clear that his studies of past campaigns waged on Vietnamese soil provided a mirror of the future for Giap. While he was interested in obtaining the most modern weapons available, he was also determined that they should not dominate military thinking in the sense that technique should be considered the decisive factor. People must always hold the first place in military planning, but they should also be given the best weapons available. Courage and a readiness for sacrifice was essential for an army determined to win, but courage used with intelligence; sacrifice as sparingly as possible.

One of the aspects of the Le Loi victory which greatly impressed Giap was Nguyen Trai's 'better win hearts than citadels' idea. This concept was reformulated by the United States as 'winning hearts and minds', on which many millions of dollars were uselessly spent in Vietnam. The fact that several towns, over 100,000 Chinese soldiers and tens of thousands of Vietnamese troops pressed into Chinese service, had surrendered due to the 'persuasion' work initiated by Nguyen Trai, was considered by Giap as a fact of capital importance, as can be seen from his writings on the Le Loi campaign. Also the fact that what had started out as a nation-wide insurrection against a local tyrant had developed into a

42

full-fledged war of national liberation, during which the 'troops of the just cause' developed into a main army. He considered that this period gave birth to elements of People's War which he was later to develop to such a high degree of perfection. It was no accident, therefore, that the official name of the offensive which ended the war in 1975 was 'The Spring 1975 General Offensive and People's Uprisings', which was a correct definition of the campaign waged.

If one can ever postulate such a contradiction in terms as the 'humanization of war', Nguyen Trai was a pioneer in the field. And his twentieth-century descendants followed his example. Destruction of the enemy forces is obviously the major aim of any military commander. Morally, it is less easy to implement enthusiastically when the enemy are of your own blood. It was a question I raised with General Van Tien Dung, Field Commander of The 1975 Spring Offensive, by asking what was the most difficult decision he had to make during that whirlwind campaign that ended the war.

A short, stocky, cheerful person – a Hanoi textile worker until he joined Giap and the others to wage revolutionary war – he was prompt to reply: 'How to take Saigon with minimum bloodshed.' He explained the necessity of absolutely crushing the Saigon Army and administration and doing it quickly before the rainy season started. 'This would have held up further military operations for months and opened the way to all sorts of diplomatic initiatives which we would have welcomed earlier but which would now be attempts to salvage a Saigon régime already condemned to defeat. We had to smash with one decisive blow the military machine set up by the United States. But how to do this with the minimum human and material destruction? This was one of the most difficult problems to solve. Also deciding what to do with the many hundreds of thousands of soldiers in the enemy ranks. They were Vietnamese, most of them ordinary people, wanting nothing better than to return to their families, their jobs or studies.

'We were all agreed that the comparative handful of leaders who insisted on fighting to the bitter end had to be stamped out. We considered that most of them would flee at the last moment anyway, as they did. But we wanted to offer a way out for the rank and file without further blood-letting. Hundreds of thousands of them would become decent, useful citizens and help to build up a prosperous life for the country and their families. So the difficult decision we finally took was to strike with utmost speed and overwhelming force right at the heart of enemy power in Saigon while instructing our political organizations there to step up to the utmost their work of persuasion among enemy troops.'

From the very beginning of the war against the French in 1945, in every military, political and psychological operation, one could see this cross-fertilization of ideas linking the past with the present. One had the impression of the historian-warrior Giap patiently sifting through all the seeds of the past to find those that could usefully be planted for the present and future. And not only Giap. As this was a fundamental line of Ho Chi Minh, everyone engaged in military and political planning was required to study, above all, the experience of their ancestors. They studied Marx and Lenin also, but, most importantly, their own unique and infinitely rich experience of a small nation continually in conflict with incomparably more powerful ones. It is this which made highly absurd the professional 'Vietnam-watchers' who tried to measure, by the turn of a phrase or the travel itinerary of Hanoi's leaders, who was pro-Moscow, who pro-Peking. They were all one hundred per cent pro-Vietnam, and for them the question on any given issue was whether Moscow or Peking was being pro-Vietnam. Their past, they rightly felt, gave them the right to have their own line, their own policies, strategies and tactics. 'Many thanks comrades for your most precious advice which we will most carefully study', was the attitude to counsel from their most high-powered friends, but the emphasis was on 'study' and not on application. It was thus that even in the most difficult situations the leadership retained the decision-making powers entirely in their own hands in military, political and diplomatic affairs. Much of the value of reading Giap's analysis of his ancestors' handling of such matters is in discovering how well their stubbornly defended insistence on doing things their way was justified.

44

In this respect the appreciation of Giap and other historians of the Le Loi-Nguyen Trai handling of post-war problems is fascinating:

After victory, Le Loi ordered the confiscation of all lands belonging to Ming functionaries, traitors and to Tran princes and dignitaries who had died or gone away. State lands were partly exploited by the administration itself, partly distributed to dignitaries and mandarins. But as distinct from the Tran estate owners, the mandarin land recipients could only collect land rent, but not do as they pleased with the peasants as individuals, who were subject to the direct authority of the State . . . [This was a direct blow at serfdom and warlordism based on private armies.] The Le kings paid great attention to the development of agricultural production. Lands left fallow during the years of war were quickly put under cultivation, while the State diligently set up state farms on uncultivated lands . . . Individuals were also encouraged to open up virgin lands. New lands thus came into production in the highlands and in the silted-up coastal regions. Dykes were kept in good repair and, in cases of emergency, students as well as army men were mobilized to put them back into good shape. Soldiers and Court personnel were sent in rotation to the fields to work. Harvests and cattle were especially protected. This policy greatly encouraged agricultural production and no serious famines broke out during the whole of the 15th century . . . [2]

I asked General Van Tien Dung how his officers and men felt about being switched from battlefields and training grounds to building roads and railways, digging canals, growing rice and pineapples and scores of other non-military tasks. He replied: 'There is a tradition in our country going back for many centuries for the armed forces to play a dual role in defence and production. But wherever they are – in the field or forests or on irrigation projects – the VPA officers and men never lose sight of their main role, defence of the

2. *Vietnam: A Historical Sketch*, op cit, pp 72–3.

Fatherland. Diverting large forces into productive work does not hamper us in building up our armed forces into a really strong, modern force.'

This historical continuity of so many aspects of Vietnamese life is one of the secrets of the smooth transition from a wartime to peacetime order. From battlefields back to ricefields seemed a normal development for hundreds of thousands of Vietnamese because they knew that was the way it had always been. History had conditioned them for this, which is why it is impossible to understand anything that happens in Vietnam without delving into some of the fundamental elements of their history. In Giap's evaluation of the post-war policies of Le Loi and Nguyen Trai (*Armement des Masses Révolutionnaires*, etc.) he notes with approval the measures taken to strengthen the three-tier military system, introduced by the Ly and Tran dynasties by creating a Court army at the central level, regional troops and those at village level. Drawing appropriate conclusions from the defection of many of the feudal lords – together with the mercenary troops in their service – Giap writes that the system under which the 'grand seigneurs' had their private armies was abolished and that all three categories of troops came under a centralized command. This was a heavy blow at the traditional feudal order of society as it functioned anywhere in the world, eliminating – at least during Le Loi's lifetime – the risk of secession and warlordism which plagued China throughout so much of its history. Universal military service was therefore restored.

In the latter half of the fifteenth century, when England and France were recovering from the Hundred Years' War and Christopher Columbus was discovering the 'New World', including America, and the Portuguese – hard on the heels of their famous navigators and fleets of caravels – were starting to colonize America, Vietnam was an advanced feudal state, at least organizationally and culturally. In 1483, the Hung Duc Code, a form of constitution, was introduced and remained in force for the next three hundred years. It is characteristic of the Vietnamese that they never 'threw the baby out with the bath water'. Although they repeatedly threw out the feudal Chinese, they retained what was positive. The retention of Chinese ideographs to serve as a written form for their own language was a case in point, also the retention of a modified form of Confucianism as an official state ideology. A form of the Chinese educational system through periodic literary contests for all candidates for public office was also retained until the French threw it out.

The Hung Duc Code, of six chapters and 721 articles, was firmly based on Confucian concepts. Reactionary as many of these were, the codification of laws and customs that had survived the centuries was, for its day, an advanced contribution to the rule of law. But typically Confucian was the definition of the most serious of ten capital crimes as disobedience to the king, closely followed by neglect of filial duties. The authority of the father, first wife and eldest son were specified, also the sanctity of private ownership of land – but not ownership of the peasants as formerly – by landlords and the State. A notable improvement on codified laws in Vietnam at the time was protection for certain rights of women, including equal rights of inheritance and repudiation of a husband in case of prolonged desertion. (Under the nineteenth-century Nguyen dynasty, however, the provisions were abolished and the plight of women became worse than before.)

Within the zigs and zags of Vietnam's feudal era, the fifteenth century marked a high point. However contradictory it may seem Confucianism waxed as Chinese influence waned. It was certain humanist and practical aspects of Confucianism that Vietnamese scholars found most attractive, whereas the notion of unqualified support for the monarch and the strict, hierarchical rules of filial piety were found irksome. At the beginning of the sixteenth century the Le dynasty, and with it the feudal system, began to decline. As in all prolonged periods without foreign invasions, the cement that held national unity together began to crumble. The feudal lords began to cast off the restrictions which Le Loi and Nguyen Trai had imposed on their powers and privileges. Struggles for dominance started between the most powerful of them, and the peasants renewed their perpetual struggle against the oppressive practices of the landlords. Armed struggle between various clans reached its climax in that between the Trinh and the Nguyen.

Although both claimed they were defending the Le dynasty, the result was that they set up rival régimes, the Trinh in the north with their capital in Thanh Long (Hanoi), the Nguyen in the south with Hue as their capital, dividing the country in the mid seventeenth century between the seventeenth and eighteenth parallels. Each side built parallel walls running east from the fishing port of Dong Hoi to the Laotian frontier. With the country divided territorially and riven by internal dissensions within each of the two halves, it was a situation badly in need of a hero. He was found in the form of Nguyen Hue, whom history knows better as King Quang Trung.

CHAPTER 5

THE TAY SON AND SAIGON

Warming to the subject closest to his heart – the role of the peasantry in Vietnamese history – Vo Nguyen Giap describes the background to what became known as the Tay Son insurrection. Tay Son was the village in the South from which Nguyen Hue, and his two brothers (not to be confused with Nguyen rulers in the South) originated.

Starting from the sixteenth century the feudal state started to decline. For over 200 years the feudal forces had been at each other's throats. Civil war between the Trinh and the Mac lasted over half a century, that between the Trinh and the Nguyen, which lasted almost as long, led to the country's partition for over a century. The feudal leaders oppressed and exploited the peasantry in an outrageous fashion. Fearing popular uprisings they confiscated firearms and [banned] their manufacture by the population. Peasant struggles were ferociously repressed by the army. Insurrections and large-scale jacqueries [peasant revolts] constantly broke out, notably in the eighteenth century. The uprising of the Tay Son, led by Nguyen Hue, represented the culminating point of these. This uprising marked a new development of insurrection and war in the co-ordination between the armed masses and the armed forces. Originally a peasant movement, it developed into a national movement. Whilst the decadent feudal class had capitulated before the aggressor, the banner of national salvation passed into the hands of Nguyen Hue, an outstanding leader of the peasant movement.

Thus the peasant insurrections and the national wars were animated by a new and vigorous spirit. At the very beginning of the uprising the slogan: 'Take from the rich to give to the poor' had inspired the peasants and other under-privileged classes to rise up. The armed forces of the peasant insurrection, before this was transformed into a national war, were built up from the 'troops of the just cause' and gradually became the army, with the large-scale participation of the peasantry and other sectors of the population.

The first 'troops of the just cause' of the Tay Son were quite clearly an armed organization of the poor masses of the population – peasants, handicraft workers and others – who provided themselves with different types of arms: cudgels, lances, pikes, swords, firearms, etc. Wherever the troops of Nguyen Hue went, peasants and other sectors of the population rose up to do the same thing, to enlarge the ranks and overthrow the decadent feudal power. It was an army of peasants which was transformed into the national army. Its organization, as well as its armament, attained a very high level of development.[1]

Under the Trinh régime in the North ,the expropriation of lands by a landowning class, which had gradually emerged through custom and laws regarding inheritance, by the aristocracy and mandarins (who had again acquired the automatic right to land because of their status), proceeded apace. The chronic contradiction between population growth and scarcity of arable land, which has plagued North Vietnam ever since, made itself felt with increasing urgency. The beginning of the

1. *Armément des Masses Révolutionnaires, Edification de l'Armée du Peuple*, op cit, pp 73–5.

50

eighteenth century was a period in which the peasant small-owners were bamboozled by floods of legal documents which, in the name of protecting their land-holding rights, were in fact instruments of their expropriation, and once again the traditional communal lands were an object of high-level land-grabbing at the expense of the villagers.

All this, not surprisingly, led to a disintegration of rural society. Irrigation works fell into disrepair, expropriated peasants having neither interest nor physical strength to expend their labour power on maintenance work, especially with corrupt local officials pocketing the money allocated for such works. Natural calamities, too, which throughout the centuries had been vigorously fought against by the peasantry, now took their course, resulting in uncontrolled floods, drought and famine.

South of the Dong Hoi wall, despite the greater abundance of land and a far more generous climate, the situation for the peasantry was little better. The more and better the land, the more voracious the appetites of the feudal lords and the greater the rivalry between them to have the best slices of the pie. The remnants of the Champa Empire had almost been digested before the partition and the Nguyens completed the process. Later, taking advantage of in-fighting among the Khmers of the Mekong delta and on the pretext of having been invited to help one faction against the other, the Nguyens took over what was later known as Cochin-Chine – mainly the Mekong delta. (Westerners who started arriving in the eighteenth century gave the name Cochin-Chine to the whole territory governed by the Nguyen, but distinguished between Lower Cochin-Chine – the Mekong delta – and the rest up to the Dong Hoi wall which they called Upper Cochin-Chine.)

Just as many Chinese fled south to escape the recurrent invasions from their north, so Vietnamese also fled south to escape the wars which raged between the Trinh and the Nguyen (1627–72) and the taxes, conscription and forced labour which fed those wars. The Red river delta in the north was over-crowded even in those days whereas the coastal plains leading south and the well-watered lands of the Mekong delta were rich and under-populated, a matter that neither rice-growing

51

Vietnamese peasants nor their feudal lords were likely to overlook.

A remarkable eighteenth-century Vietnamese historian and encyclopaedist, Le Quy Don – a one-time provincial governor and ambassador to China, and critical observer of the contemporary scene – whose published works run to over one hundred volumes, listing in detail the annual extortions in cash, gold and silver by the Nguyen lords, drily noted: 'For every amount the State collected, the mandarin-collectors took twice as much for themselves.' Also that: 'Since the start of the reign of Vo Vuong (1738), luxury prevailed, petty mandarins imitating higher officials. Houses were sculptured, walls built of stone, hangings and curtains made of silk, plates and dishes of bronze or porcelain, the furniture of precious wood. Harnesses were ornamented with gold and silver ... They regarded gold and silver as sand; rice as dirt...'[2]

Corruption was rampant, too, and even the office of mandarin, traditionally rigorously controlled through the competitive examination system, could now be had by bribery. This applied in the North also. Such were the conditions, therefore, which provoked a whole series of peasant revolts, north and south of the Dong Hoi wall – including a notable one led by a Buddhist monk in the North. Many of them were spontaneous uprisings in which starving, dispossessed peasants simply stormed the towns in search of food. Rigorous security measures – some of which were a foretaste of those tried out in the south by the Saigon dictatorships 200 years later – failed, however, to stem the tide of revolt.

Among several revolts which took place, one in Hai Duong, in 1739, lasted just thirty years, the insurgent troops moving from place to place, practising guerilla warfare and holding their own with the Trinh regular army; disappearing in one province only to turn up in another. But all these revolts, north and south of the Dong Hoi line, were but a preview of great things to come. In 1771, Nguyen Nhac, a minor tax collector of Tay Son village in the south-central coastal province of Binh Dinh, together with his two brothers, Hue and Lu, launched the uprising which enters history as the Tay

2. *Vietnam· A Historical Sketch*, op cit, p 106.

52

Son rebellion. (By one of those quirks of history, the Nguyen brothers unfurled their banner of revolt just eighty years before the T'ai P'ing peasant rebellion with similar aims, slogans, tactics and even mystique, swept China. Probably taking western missionaries too literally, the Tay Sons and the T'ai P'ings both claimed they were envoys from Heaven, fighting to establish a 'Heaven on Earth'.) Who would know better about the 'hell on earth' in his native province, than tax collector Nguyen Nhac? As in all such cases, the peasants flocked to join the 'troops of the just cause'. Within two years the provinces of Quang Ngai and Quang Nam were in the hands of the Tay Sons, bringing them very close to the Dong Hoi line. Taking advantage of the weakening of their rivals, the Trinh invaded from the North, seizing the capital of the Nguyen lords and forcing them to flee further south. Shrewd political, as well as military, tacticians, the brothers negotiated a temporary agreement with the Trinh, while they took over the rest of both Upper and Lower Cochin-Chine, wiping out the Nguyens and distributing land as they went. By 1778, virtually the whole of what later became known as South Vietnam was in the hands of the Tay Son brothers. Nguyen Nhac proclaimed himself king, setting up his capital at Do Ban, in his native Binh Dinh.

One of the Nguyen lords – Nguyen Anh – however, had escaped with a large number of troops, to a remote part of the Mekong delta. Mounting a temporarily successful counter-offensive, his forces were then completely crushed and Nguyen Anh fled to Phu Quoc island in the Gulf of Siam. From there he committed a crime till then unprecedented in Vietnamese history. He called in foreign help, in the form of the Siamese, and started Vietnam again down the slippery slope of foreign domination. In the past foreign invaders had pushed their way in uninvited. This time they were invited. However, although the Siamese monarchy provided Nguyen Anh with an army of 20,000 men and 300 vessels, the 1784 invasion of the western part of the Mekong delta was a failure, the attack being successfully repulsed by Nguyen Hue.

Having dealt with Nguyen Anh and the threat from Siam, Nguyen Hue turned his attentions to the Trinhs in the North, proclaiming his intention to restore the Le dynasty to its rightful status. This he speedily accomplished and, as a reward, received the hand of King Le Hien Tong's daughter in marriage. The country was reunited, the Le dynasty restored to power, the peasants were back on their lands, many of their grievances had been redressed during the course of the armed struggle. Nguyen Hue could return with his bride, Ngoc Han, to his native Binh Dinh province, and enjoy the peace he had fought so valiantly to restore and the bliss of married life. Peace for another 'ten thousand generations'! So it must have seemed at the time.

In fact the greatest trials still lay ahead. King Le Hien Tong died and his successor, Le Chieu Tong, egged on by notables and mandarins disgruntled by the drastic pruning of their estates and privileges by the Tay Son brothers, turned against them. But an attempted counter-revolutionary coup was a failure, the ring-leaders were captured and executed. King Le Chieu Tong fled the capital, but compounded the treachery of Nguyen Anh by inviting Emperor Chen Lung, of China's Ch'ing (Manchu) dynasty to invade the country and restore him to the throne. Chen Lung was only too happy to oblige and thus, in October 1788, an army of 200,000 Manchu troops invaded from the north, entering Thanh Long just one month later to set up Le Chieu Thong as the puppet 'King of Annam', with the real power being exercised by Chen Lung's pro-consul, General Sun Tchei-y. Another of those recurrent monumental crises in Vietnam's history was at hand.

Nguyen Hue acted swiftly, firstly by denouncing the Le dynasty and proclaiming himself the new king – Quang Trung – and secondly, on 21 December 1788, by putting himself at the head of an army of 100,000 men to march on Thanh Long. It was seven months before the French people stormed the Bastille to have an accounting with *their* feudal régime and four years before Rouget de Lisle composed the Marseillaise. Vietnamese historians do not record to what tune Quang Trung and his hundred thousand marched on Thanh Long! But they do record that in reviewing his troops during a rest at Nghe An on 26 December, the Tay Son commander declared:

54

The Ch'ing have invaded our country, occupied the capital city of Thanh Long. In our history, the Trung sisters fought against the Han; Dinh Tien Hoang against the Sung; Tran Hung Dao against the Mongols; Le Loi against the Ming. Those heroes did not resign themselves to standing by and seeing the invaders plunder our country. They roused the people up to fight for the just cause and drive out the aggressors . . . The Ch'ing, forgetting what happened to the Sung, the Mongols and the Ming, have invaded our country. We are going to drive them out of our territory . . .[3]

He also promised his troops that they would celebrate the seventh day of the Lunar New Year, 1789, in Thanh Long. So, after a ten-day rest at Nghe An to build up his force, Nguyen Hue advanced on Thanh Long, attacking the capital with three columns from the south and west. The rapidity of the advance took the Ch'ing commanders by surprise – a lesson that Giap also took to heart – and their defeat was total. One of the three key post commanders hanged himself; Commander-in-Chief Sun Hsi-y – whom legend has it was amusing himself with his concubines at the moment of the assault by Nguyen Hue's elephant-mounted troops – had neither time to put on his armour nor to have his horse harnessed before dashing for the pontoon bridge over the Red river erected less than three months earlier for his triumphant entry into the capital. He set the example for a panic-stricken flight, and history records that many of the survivors of the initial attacks were drowned in the general stampede to get across the Red river and on the way back to China. Thus in six days, the Tay Son troops had advanced 80 kms, defeated an army comprising 200,000 men, and celebrated victory on the seventh day of the Lunar New Year, in Thanh Long.

In the south, Nguyen Anh had not been idle. Taking advantage of Nguyen Hue's drive against the Ch'ings in the north and the inefficiency of his two brothers – Nguyen Lu based at Gia Dinh and charged with governing Cochin-Chine and

3. *Vietnam: A Historical Sketch*, op cit, p 112.

Nguyen Nhac in Hue to govern Annam – Nguyen Anh and his troops seized Gia Dinh.[4]

In 1792 King Quang Trung died, after having carried out very important administrative reforms and others aimed at putting the peasants back on the land and at reviving agriculture and handicrafts. He left a son of ten years – Quang Toan – as his successor. Nguyen Nhac died the following year, leaving the weakest of the three, Nguyen Lu, as the sole survivor of the Tay Son brothers. By this time, Nguyen Anh was already in contact with the French through the Catholic missionaries and had secured French advisers and military equipment for his armed forces. From Gia Dinh, he gradually pushed north against Tay Son forces, demoralized by the loss of their main leaders and without a firm guiding hand. On 1 June 1802, when it was clear that victory was in sight, Nguyen Anh proclaimed himself king, taking the name Gia Long, leading his troops into Thanh Long on 20 July the same year as the founder of the Nguyen dynasty. A whole historic period had come to a close and a new period of western colonialism was about to be ushered in.

Vo Nguyen Giap's views of the achievements of the Tay Son are very significant and there is little doubt that the Giap–Dung strategy and tactics in the final days of their offensive were inspired by Nguyen Hue's drive on Thanh Long two hundred years earlier. Indeed, there was no more able hand than that of Vo Nguyen Giap to pick up the torch of national resistance where Nguyen Hue had left it. His admiration for Nguyen Hue's lightning tactics inspired the instructions with which Giap, as Minister of Defence and Commander-in-Chief of the VPA, bombarded his Chief-of-Staff and Field

4. Gia Dinh, which roughly corresponds to today's Saigon, in those days was an administrative district with an important citadel. At the end of the seventeenth century, large numbers of Chinese – fleeing from South China as the Ch'ings gradually consolidated the southern part of their kingdom – were allowed to take up land in Gia Dinh. Construction of the port of Saigon was started by the Tay Son in 1777, including big canals linking the Saigon river with the Mekong delta. But even in 1815, maps show that Saigon was mainly a single street linking the port area with Cholon (Big Market) which had developed into a mainly Chinese-occupied trading centre. Later Gia Dinh became the province in which the then three separate towns, Saigon, Gia Dinh and Cholon were situated.

Commander, General Van Tien Dung, as the revolutionary forces closed in on Saigon in 1975. How could obepience to such insistent orders be combined with overall policy of keeping losses – civilian and for the military of both sides – to the minimum. It was another question I put to the smiling and relaxed General Van Tien Dung two years later, in his Hanoi headquarters. Before he replied, he looked at his date watch, and said: 'By the way, today is the second anniversary of one of the great dates of the war for those of us who were directing the campaign. It was on 14 April, two years ago, that the Political Bureau cabled acceptance of our suggestion that the battle for Saigon should be called "Operation Ho Chi Minh". Once that was decided everybody knew that we would throw in everything. A few days later the first tropical storms started and we knew we had really to hurry. Once the name of the operation was agreed we pledged to liberate Saigon for Ho Chi Minh's birthday – 19 May. But in our hearts we knew we had to act faster, beat the calendar and the rains.' What are the possibilities of 'dash', 'verve', and 'single blows' under such circumstances and how does a field commander plan such an operation involving the movement of hundreds of thousands of men from all points of the compass?

'The detailed answer you will find in this book,' replied Van Tien Dung, handing me an autographed copy in Vietnamese of his book *Dai Than Mua Xuan* (The Spring Offensive) (Hanoi, 1976). But he also gave me a thumbnail sketch which ran as follows:

In the early stages of the campaign we relied on surprise; fooling the enemy by striking where he least expected, and when he did expect us, striking in such force that he never dreamed we had. With Saigon it was different. Your colleagues, the journalists, had anticipated the direction of our thrust apparently before the Saigon High Command. They hinted that Saigon was an imminent target shortly after we had made the decision. Saigon and the Americans believed we would not dare. It must be for next year. But some foreign journalists had rather accurately guessed at not only the direction of our thrust but also the strength of our forces. Having lost the advantage of surprise in these two aspects we had to try for a still greater surprise effect – the timing and the rapidity of the operation.

To direct the operation, Van Tien Dung and his staff, later joined by Le Duc Tho, veteran of so many diplomatic duels with Henry Kissinger, representing the Communist Party's Political Bureau, and Pham Hung, Chief Political Officer of the VPA, moved into a forward headquarters in the famous 'Iron Triangle' area, a little over twenty miles from Saigon. From maps and detailed reports of underground cadres from Saigon, they familiarized themselves with boulevards, streets, buildings – including their length, breadth and height – the width and depth of rivers and canals, the approaches of bridges, the composition and morale of the enemy units assigned to defend the city, the political leanings, the characters and habits of unit commanders. Neither Van Tien Dung nor his closest aides had ever been in Saigon, but, as he expressed it: 'We soaked in all this information to an extent that in every waking and sleeping moment, I was literally haunted by the topography of Saigon. Bit by bit the locations of roads and canals, bridges, storage depots, administrative and military centres became engraved in my mind.' He continued:

> Finally we chose five priority targets. The General Staff Headquarters, the Presidential Palace, the Special Capital Command Headquarters,[5] the Police Headquarters and Tan Son Nhut airport. These were the key centres of civil and military power, the essential cogs of the military and repressive machinery; the places where the élite of national treason were continuing to work on plans for continuing the war. Lightning blows there would topple the whole edifice, army and administration would be like a serpent with its head lopped off; the whole defensive system and repressive machinery would collapse, the

5. Apart from the four Zonal Military Headquarters, or 1, 2, 3 and 4 Corps areas, there was a special command set up for the defence of the Saigon area which had its headquarters in Saigon.

masses would rise up and no force, no individual would be able to do anything about it. The decisive strategic battle would be short, Saigon rapidly liberated.

There was no other solution if we wanted to save the lives of over $3\frac{1}{2}$ million people in Saigon and avoid the destruction of the economic, cultural and social infrastructure. To do this we would have to break through five divisions guarding the approaches and deal with 100,000 troops and para-military units inside the city. The main thing would be to dash straight ahead for the main targets.

That this very unorthodox strategy succeeded, the Saigon defenders being completely staggered by the speed and strength of the five-pronged attack – a prong for every target – is certainly remarkable. It was also done in defiance of any textbook rules, but by methods which Nguyen Hue would surely have applauded. Saigon was taken intact with not more than a few hundred casualties on both sides and hardly a civilian scratched. Nguyen Hue would have surely praised the fact that Saigon was liberated twenty days before the promised date!

CHAPTER 6

A NATION OF POETS

The door to the French invasion of Indochina
had been partly opened by Nguyen Anh in 1787, when he
sent his son – escorted by the French missionary, Bishop
Pigneau de Béhaine – to persuade Louis XVI to send military
help to Nguyen Anh in his fight against the Tay Son brothers.
A treaty was actually signed on 28 November 1787, between
Bishop de Béhaine, on behalf of Nguyen Anh, and a representative of the French crown, under which France would supply
military aid in exchange for use of the port of Tourane
(Danang), and the island of Con Son, known later as Poulo
Condor, one of the world's most infamous penal settlements
under French and American control. France would also be
the only European state to enjoy free trading rights with
Vietnam. At a time when France was competing with Britain
to get into China through the southern back door, this was a
highly advantageous deal for France.

The storming of the Bastille twenty months later, however,
put a temporary halt to this, and within four years Louis XVI
lost his head for precisely what Nguyen Anh was doing,
negotiating with a foreign power (Austria in the case of
Louis XVI) for help in putting down a revolutionary uprising
in order to preserve his throne and feudal power. The best
the Bishop de Béhaine could do was to pass the hat around

among French merchants, who had already established a trading foothold in the south, to buy some arms and pay some mercenaries to be placed at the disposal of Nguyen Anh.

It was more than half a century after the French Revolution before France, under Louis Philippe, again took notice of Vietnam and the treaty signed with Nguyen Anh, who, after reigning as Emperor Gia Long, had already died. A preliminary attempt to move into Tourane in April 1847, however, was resisted and French warships sank five Vietnamese armoured junks in the harbour. There would undoubtedly have been a follow-up action had not France been rocked by its 1848 revolution ten months later, during which Louis Philippe 'King of the French' was overthrown and forced to cross the Channel into exile. It was not until Louis Napoleon (Napoleon III) of the Second Empire had consolidated his position that France, in August 1858, seriously set about the conquest of Vietnam – again starting with Tourane.

Into what sort of people had the Vietnamese developed during all those centuries of struggle? We have seen them as dour, stoical fighters, desperately intent on defending the only territory they knew. As they were not of migrant origin, there was no 'home country' to return to when oppression or foreign domination became too intolerable. And after Cochin-Chine had been colonized there were simply no lands further south to which to migrate. We have seen them so far as tillers of the soil and capable of great sacrifices and much heroism in defending that soil. But what was the quality of their life at the time the French arrived?

They were highly educated people and those most venerated by the people were the scholars. Under the Vietnamese variant of Confucianism, filial piety meant loyalty first to the king, then to the teacher, then to the father. There was a very strong bond between scholars and people, the best of the scholars almost invariably preferring to live in the villages than in the towns. Their roots also went deep into their native soil which helps explain, as will be noted later, their role in the patriotic struggles against the French. It is of historical significance that within a century of Vietnam winning its independence from China, King Ly Thanh Ton built the beautiful Temple of Literature, which still stands in Hanoi. Its functions were partly those of a tribune for the triennial mandarin competitions at which the highly prized doctorates in literature were awarded, partly those of a higher educational institution where sons of leading dignitaries were trained in Confucian ethics which they were expected to abide by in their administrative duties.

In the struggle between Buddhism – Vietnam's first religion, introduced via China and India – and Confucianism, the scholars sided with the latter. Reactionary as it was as a concept, it nevertheless dealt with practical things on this earth, laying down rules under which society should be governed, whereas Buddhism stressed the unreality of this world and, like the Christian religion, directed men's thoughts to the next one with much accent on securing a place there by one's behaviour on earth. Historian Dr Nguyen Khac Vien maintains there was a 'dividing line' in the thirteenth century between the Vietnamese aristocracy and the Buddhist clergy on the one hand, and the Confucian scholars defending the rights of peasants, serfs and slaves on the other. The scholars, basing themselves on Confucian precepts to defend the oppressed rural population among whom they lived, developed a vigorous literature based on denouncing the corruption of the Buddhist hierarchy and the waste associated with the interminable building of pagodas and monasteries. Early feminist writers even questioned the hypocritical sexual habits of the 'ascetic' Buddhist bonzes. In the early fourteenth century, Truong Han Sieu a former deputy foreign minister turned writer, described the bonzes as

Scoundrels who had lost all notion of Buddhist asceticism and only thought of possessing beautiful monasteries and gardens, building luxurious residences, surrounding themselves with hosts of servants . . . People became monks by the thousands, so as to get food without having to plough and clothes without having to weave. They deceived the people, undermined morality, squandered riches, were all over the place, followed by numerous believers; very few of them were not real bandits![1]

It was the sort of attack that Oliver Cromwell was to make in the House of Commons 300 years later against the leaders of the established religion of his day. While there were never any religious wars in Vietnam, Confucianism clearly won out not only as the proclaimed official doctrine but that which was popularly accepted as the guide to daily life. And it was this doctrine which dominated the highly developed Vietnamese educational system. To justify to their own people the costs of conquest, the French resorted to the rationalization of all colonial powers in such cases by stressing the 'civilizing nature' of their enterprise. They were bringing not only the blessings of Christianity to 'pagans' but also those of French civilization, including the French language and education. In fact the Vietnamese could have given the French some useful lessons in civilization, and even taught them something about education.

In 1952, an internationally renowned French-educated Vietnamese scholar and poet, Huynh Khac Dung, wrote a series of essays on the subject of education in Vietnam as it had existed for many centuries up until the arrival of the French in the mid nineteenth century. They were published in the conservative Saigon monthly, *France-Asie*, and later issued in summarized form in a special supplement. The founder-editor of *France-Asie*, Réne de Berval, to whom I am indebted for permission to quote from what represents a synthesis of many years of research, by way of introduction praised Huynh Khac Dung for having 'applied himself to probing into the very essence of [Vietnam's] national culture . . . not only a literary success but one of human effort – by transforming astonishment into evidence . . .' This was an honest scholarly admission by René de Berval, which must have aroused some ire in official French circles in Saigon. There were, indeed, grounds for astonishment when the author, in his well-documented work, maintained that it was France which introduced illiteracy into Vietnam. He starts by pointing

1. *Vietnam: A Historical Sketch*, op cit, p 55.

64

out that until the beginning of the present century, Vietnam's culture was deeply influenced by that of China:

In our country, so long closed to all western civilization, the world of literature enjoyed a preponderant role in social as well as political life, merging in fact with the official world. Education, very freely available, though not compulsory, was the best proof of the importance attached to this. It was not at all the privilege of a restricted élite, but of the whole people. Illiteracy was an exception. The peasant who laboured all day long under a hot sun could be sufficiently educated to draw up a sales contract, a mortgage or any other such document. The housewife who rocked her baby in a hammock, or bent under the September rains to plant out rice seedlings in the fields, and the tradesman who peddled his merchandise all the year round in the village streets, in their leisure hours they could be devotees of the muses. But can one say that this passion for literature was innate, disinterested? I fear not. The considerable esteem lavished on education can be explained by the undeniable truth that graduation in literature led to public office, that is to comfort, glory. In short, the average Vietnamese knew that education was a necessity, an advantageous condition in the struggle for life, a source of strength in a society of omnipotent and arbitrary mandarins, the 'mother-and-father' of the people. [2]

The author goes on to explain that there were two types of basic education at village level, that given by official teachers, or *huan dao*, and that given by *thay do* (schoolmasters) who did not require any teaching diplomas. At district and provincial level, education was dispensed by officially diplomaed teachers, known as *giao-tho* and *doc-hoc*, the latter in charge of education at provincial level. Above these school institutions, which were open to all, was the Quoc-tu-giam (Imperial

2. This and subsequent quotes from Huynh Khac Dung are translated by the author from Huynh Khac Dung's *L'Enseignement dans l'Ancien Vietnam* (Saigon, 1952).

College), directed by a *tu-nghiep* (High Civil Mandarin). This college prepared the literary competitions and at the top of the hierarchy was the *Han-lam-vien* (Imperial Academy) which was in charge of overall supervision.

Primary school pupils started with the *Book in Three Characters* comprising texts in three-word lines that were easy to memorize and had been in use since Vietnam won its independence in the tenth century. Huynh Khac Dung explains that it introduced the pupils to the 'three great powers of nature' (heaven, earth and man, in that order), preparing them for the more complicated texts of Confucius and his main disciples. Even these rhymes laid much emphasis on filial piety, self-perfection and moral rectitude. As students climbed up the ladder of learning, studies included the Chinese historical Annals dating back to over 2000 BC; the Vietnamese historical Annals covering the period from tenth-century independence to Nguyen Anh's seizure of power at the beginning of the nineteenth century; the main Confucian classics; and a collection of over 300 poems, folk songs, legends and other literary works, some of which dated back to 1700 BC.

The pupils, whether studying under private or official teachers, could present themselves at four different levels of examinations, the lowest being held annually at provincial level. The subject was a dissertation on literature presented in prose or verse. Those who passed won the right to present themselves for examinations at the next highest level and were exempted from corvée (forced unpaid labour) for one year. The next level was a test as to the worthiness of candidates to compete at the next highest level for a bachelor's or master's degree. The eliminating examination was held at the provincial level every three years, the contests for the degrees also taking place only once in three years. In the strictly codified order of things the triennial examinations had to coincide with the lunar years of the Rat, the Cat, the Horse or the Cock.

The literary contests were great national events and Huynh Khac Dung explains that the whole country was divided into 'five literary regions', each including several provinces. Contests for the degrees were held in the 'capital' of the literary

66

region in which the candidates resided. The competitions comprised four tests, and candidates were eliminated at each of them. Only the notes 'good' and 'very good' obtained in the preceding examinations allowed candidates to present themselves for the fourth.

According to the mentions received, the successful candidates in the third examination were classified as having received their degree of master or bachelor. Each was presented with a silk gown from the Emperor and took part in various celebrations at the Temple of Literature. The third level of examinations selected those who could be admitted to compete in the triennial ones, held in the Imperial Palace for those aspiring to the degree of doctor. It was during this preliminary selection for the highest of scholastic honours that literary ability and potential administrative capacity began to mix. Apart from examination in classical literary subjects and composing poems and works of prose, the candidates had to edit an Imperial edict, write a memorandum or report addressed to the Emperor by a mandarin and make a dissertation on a philosophical theme.

No degrees were awarded to those who succeeded; their reward was the right to sustain a thesis proposed by the Emperor who – with two examiner assistants – judged the quality of the theses and decided on the classification of the winners. Such was the standard of achievement that only three 'doctors first class' were chosen at each contest!

Until I read Huynh Khac Dung's essays, I could never understand the awe with which Vietnamese friends would point to a village and say: 'That village produced . . . number of doctors throughout the centuries . . .' A doctor had to be a man of great erudition and, as one learns through Vietnamese history, an honourable proportion of them were also great patriots. Nguyen Trai, the political *alter ego* of Le Loi, obtained his doctorate at the early age of twenty-one. The father of Ho Chi Minh also won his doctorate, and for a short time served as a mandarin in the Court of Hue. Huynh Khac Dung, an avowed Confucian, was an enthusiast for the literary contests:

The educational system founded on the principles of

social morality had great merits. Firstly it was fundamentally democratic; it sustained the taste for, and cult of, literature; it trained officials capable of good management of public affairs. A number of them later distinguished themselves as excellent strategists, as talented economists and diplomats. Impregnated by the values of Confucian philosophy, the individual aimed at self perfection as a rule of conduct; in other words thanks to the persevering practice of Virtue, to become the Superior Man that Confucius wanted. The concept was that, based on a sum total of strict dogmas, the Confucian school had, despite social transformations, created Man satisfied with his lot, living an intense inner life without bothering about material considerations.

A satisfactory state of affairs perhaps for autocratic rulers! But the fact is that Vietnam had an organized university system from 1075 onwards which, historically considered, compared with the earliest universities in medieval Europe of the eleventh and twelfth centuries.

The whole course of Vietnamese history, however, testifies to the fact that not every Man, and especially not every Woman, were satisfied with their lot. Indeed, in the period immediately preceding the French conquest, many Vietnamese were wrestling with their Confucian-indoctrinated consciences over the compelling need to commit the ultimate of crimes – revolt against the king. And the most popular poetess of the day, Ho Xuan Hoang, was committing the second most heinous crime, by leading scathing attacks on filial piety, male domination, the system of concubinage and every other aspect of the degradation of women. Precisely because of the capitulation of Nguyen Anh (Emperor Gia Long) the revolt against authority, the greatest heresy according to Confucian precepts, attained important dimensions in the late eighteenth and early nineteenth centuries. In their selective Confucianism, however, the Vietnamese demonstrated their ability to take from foreign ideologies and philosophies that which was useful to their own needs, cultivating the positive, rejecting the negative, shaping and polishing them according to their own standards.

This was evident in the use of Chinese ideographs to develop their own language as later they were to use the Latin alphabet for the same purpose. In the same way they took what was logical, humanist and realistically ethical in the Confucian doctrines. On this latter point one can find common ground in the ethical qualities which Confucius wanted in his Superior Man and those that today's Vietnamese Communists want cultivated in what they call their New Man.

The literary contests certainly contributed to the fact that Vietnam is a nation of poets. It is a tribute to this that so many of their great heroes and leaders combined talents of statesmanship and the arts of war with those of the poet. The recurring dramas of the battles for national survival, the beauties of the country's forests, mountains, rivers and coasts – to say nothing of the people themselves, the six-tone musicality of the language, plus the thorough grounding in literary appreciation which formed the backbone of the educational system, have all combined to stimulate the cult of the poet.

Whether it is Nguyen Trai describing the defeat of the Mings; Nguyen Du in his great epic of the trials of a young beauty sold into concubinage; Ho Chi Minh penning his frustrations at his chains in Kuomintang[3] jails in China's Kwangsi province, at one of the most critical moments of the Revolution; Le Duc Tho – after leaving the Paris talks with Kissinger, following a momentous series of rapier-versus-cudgel duels – dashing off poems as he sped south to help direct the battle

3. The Kuomintang (Nationalist party) was formed by Sun Yat Sen in 1905 and mobilized liberal-progressive forces in China to overthrow the ruling dynasty in Peking and establish a republic, which was set up in 1911. Later the Kuomintang formed an alliance with the Communist Party. This was broken in 1927 when Chiang Kai-shek, brother-in-law and successor to Sun Yat Sen, turned on the Communists in 1927 in Shanghai and other places, massacring them by the tens of thousands. A Kuomintang–Communist alliance was again established early in 1937, to form a common front against the Japanese invasion of Manchuria (North-East China). At the time Ho Chi Minh was arrested, Kuomintang–Communist relations had become very strained, Chiang Kai-shek having considered that with the entry of Japan into World War II, and the acceptance of Kuomintang China into the camp of the Western Allies, he no longer needed Communist support. He saw in Ho Chi Minh and other Vietnamese nationalists, an impediment to his plans to take advantage of the weakened position of the Allies in Asia, to restore Chinese hegemony in Vietnam.

for Saigon, they, and hundreds of others, used their poetry to further the cause. Centuries of foreign domination and the particularity of the language, by which the same word may have half a dozen meanings according to the tonal inflection, developed the art of double-sense in poetry. The message was clear to a Vietnamese, but obscure to the outsider.

The works of the great poets emanate a glow of national pride; of optimism in the most hopeless of situations; of ironic humour at the barbaric clumsiness of their enemies. They reflect also the deep humanism and warm sentimentality of a people that has suffered much and takes comfort in 'small mercies'. Satire was a favourite form of deflating the mighty. An example of how an 'angry young woman', an authentic pioneer of the feminist movement 200 years ago, used her brush and ink to castigate the male-dominated society of her day, are the works of Ho Xuan Huong. Twice married, but each time as a second wife or concubine, and bitterly resenting the status of women, she wrote over sixty poems, daring in their frankness even for our own days, but how much more so in the Confucian-dominated society of her times. The following two poems are representative of her work and both appear in the *Anthologie de la Littérature Vietnamienne*, Vol 2, op cit, pp 171 and 175.

Sharing a Husband

Sharing a husband with another – what a fate!
One sleeps under well-padded blankets,
The other freezes.
By chance he grants a union,
Once or twice a month, three times nothing!
We wrangle to snatch a bowlful.
The rice is badly cooked.
I work like a servant – but unpaid,
Ah. Had I known it would be thus
I would lief have remained alone.

The Unwed Mother

A moment's pleasure – now you see me in a fine pickle,
Ah my love, can you imagine my woes?

70

The Heavens had not yet traced my fate
When a flaw already mars the willow-trunk;[4]
For a hundred years it's maybe you who bear the guilt,
For my part I agree to carry the fruit of our love.
People can say what they want, why should we care.
Well meditated or not, we were not unclever.[5]

About the time Nguyen Anh was negotiating his treachery with Bishop Pigneau de Béhaine, poet Nguyen Du was composing one of the masterpieces of world literature, the story of the fifteen years of suffering of the beautiful and talented Kieu, depicted in brilliant and moving imagery in a poem of over 3000 lines, which struck at the heart of Confucian morality. Kieu had renounced her first love and sold herself into what she thought was marriage to save her father from a debtors' prison. An excellent example of filial piety! From there she went into concubinage and prostitution, experiencing some passionate true love affairs in between. *Kieu* is the most popular Vietnamese literary work, and written in *nom* it was immediately accessible to the general public, highly literate in *nom* at the time it first appeared. Nguyen Du, from a high-ranking mandarin family and himself a mandarin until he was dismissed by the Tay Son, found a theme and a language, a heroine, heroes and villains, which came straight from the lives of the people and went straight back to their hearts. Rebels were glorified, the mighty and corrupt were castigated.

Millions of Vietnamese can quote scores of verses from *Kieu*, from the poems of Ho Xuan Huong, and from dozens of other Vietnamese poets. It is one of the reasons why they know their own history so well. When they had to un-learn the only written form of language they knew, the memorized poems were a vital element in cultural continuity.

4. A play on words which means, 'Heaven had not yet given me a husband and I'm already pregnant.'
5. Refers to an old folk proverb to the effect that to have a baby from a husband is banal, but to have no husband and produce a child is really clever. Women were the anonymous authors of many such proverbs and folk songs in their fight for sexual equality.

CHAPTER 7

WHAT THE FRENCH FOUND

'Explain yourselves' was the not very polite demand I made to Nguyen Dinh Thi, poet-novelist and soldier, whose great lyrical poem, *Song of a Hanoi-Dweller*, has made him one of the most popular contemporary writers.[1] A veteran of both resistance wars, it was in his capacity of General Secretary of the Vietnamese Union of Writers that I was speaking to him. 'How do you dare stand up to everyone? How did you dare stand up to the Americans, the Chinese and Mongols but failed against the first French invasion? And why are you all poets?' A handsome man in his early fifties with a sensitive face matching the deeply human quality of his works, he laughed, replying: 'Too many questions in one.' But he promptly launched into a lengthy and convincing explanation, the main points of which form the basis of this chapter.

He recalled that for a long time science – apart from the science of war – was very little developed. All the classical works were destroyed or removed, but it became evident the Vietnamese were strong in the science and arts of war, mostly because the feudal states were highly structured, with a military organization, administration and way of life which

1. Other works include: *The Attack* (1951), *On the Banks of the Clear River* (1956), *The Breached Dykes* (1962), *Into Fire* (1966), and *Sky Front* (1967).

existed more or less unchanged for many centuries. In addition, he stressed the great experience that his people had gained in agriculture and fishing, and because there was very little land per head, the people were required to work in a very intensive way. Rice, fish and salt provided the means for living from century to century and this was, indeed, the economic basis for waging incessant wars of national survival.

When asked why the Vietnamese peasants have always been a relatively progressive force, responsive to revolutionary ideas, taking easily to arms, and running great risks to protect cadres and generally rallying around anyone who raised the banner of revolt, he replied: 'In most countries of the world peasants are very conservative but they are less so in Vietnam. Perhaps because our peasants often had to change their place of residence. They are very attached to the soil but not exclusively to that which they have been used to tilling. Because of terrible natural calamities, or wars sweeping over their village, a change of régime and other factors, peasants become used to moving around. Attachment to the home fields and the tombs of the ancestors was very strong, but not as strong as the will to survive.'

Following on from this, I asked why so many of the intellectuals preferred the company of peasants and the rough conditions in the villages to the easier life and pleasures of the city? To this, he pointed out that the village was not only the main source of soldiers for the armed forces, it was where peasants, handicraft workers and intellectuals lived together. Towns were regarded as artificial, unnatural growths and most of the great men of letters felt infinitely more at home in the villages. Traditionally the 'great families' never meant great in any economic sense because it was intellectual and moral qualities which earned prestige. For thousands of years it continued like this – intellectuals were the cream of society whatever their economic status – because basically they came from peasant stock and felt adrift when they were cut off from their roots. Nguyen Dinh Thi felt, therefore, that it was the structure of the village as the repository of the national heritage which enabled successful resistance to foreign invasions – including that of the United States. That the French had it comparatively easy in their first invasion was because the feudal forces, in the nineteenth century, could no longer mobilize the peasantry and had to pit their classical, regular troops and their bows and arrows against French cannon.

Turning to the subject of fighting, I asked Nguyen Dinh Thi why the Vietnamese soldiers show no sign of any martial spirit or even 'Prussian' mentality, no clicking of heels and saluting of officers in the streets, nor even shouted commands on the battlefield? For him, one of the main reasons is that the Vietnamese are a gentle people whose way of life and relations with each other encourage this attitude. But the realities of life and invasions have made courage an essential if the nation was to survive. Thus, by having to do with people bigger than themselves, they have developed the quality of firmness tempered with flexibility. Using a simple analogy, Nguyen Dinh Thi takes the bamboo, the most typical vegetation over all of Vietnam, as the symbol of national character. It bends but doesn't break; strong as steel but extremely flexible. Always returning to the same position no matter how far it bends. In other words, he insisted that as a people, the Vietnamese are very proud of their independence, are jealous in protecting it, but are also open to outside influences.

On the subject of how the French administered during their colonial period and how it differed from American control, Nguyen Dinh Thi drew clear distinctions. In his own words: 'The French did not touch the basic structures, the Americans did.' The French in fact exploited the raw materials, especially human ones, by setting up large plantations for rice, coffee and rubber, using semi-slave labour. They raided villages for coolies, shaving the heads of those they rounded up and painting them different colours. Green stood for the coffee plantations, red for rubber and blue for those to be exported to their nickel mines in New Caledonia. It was to some extent these violations of human dignity that explained the violence of the August Revolution in 1945. But the French did leave the villages to themselves, and they remained more or less unchanged. The Americans, however, followed a policy of 'urbanization', which involved linking the former peasantry with the urban population. This was done through large-scale bombing of the villages, by exchange of fertilizers for rice and by using the bait of city-type gadgets. In following this policy, the Americans spent enormous sums on what was, in the end, largely unsuccessful. In fact, as Nguyen Dinh Thi said, 'in whatever physical conditions our people lived, the human relations and all the qualities of our people survived. The Americans could not destroy this in a period of ten to twenty years, although they did an enormous amount of damage. The French never understood what goes on in the minds of our people – the Americans even less.'

The French who attacked Danang on 31 August 1858, as the Americans who stormed ashore there on 4 March 1965, saw the Vietnamese as dirty, seemingly backward peasants, who apparently spent many of their daylight hours up to their knees and thighs in mud-filled fields. Most of the men were semi-naked and, especially when the French arrived, the teeth of men and women were lacquered black. This gave them a sort of permanently gaping appearance. French troops probably *did* believe they were on a 'civilizing mission' as their superiors had briefed them, in the same way the first Americans believed they were on a 'rescue mission' to repel invaders from the North.[2] In fact, at the time of the French invasion, the people who were having their insides ripped out by French grape-shot were amongst the most highly literate and civilized in the world.

In the beginning there was very little organized opposition to the French invasion. It was not by chance that the last three great resistance heroes had been Tran Hung Dao of the ruling Tran dynasty who threw out the Mongols; Le Loi – not of the feudal monarchy, but the land-owning class – aided by the

2. At the 1954 Geneva Conference on Indochina, the country had been temporarily divided along the Seventeenth Parallel, ostensibly to permit a separation of the combatants. Under the agreement the guerilla forces which had been fighting the French were to regroup their forces south of the Seventeenth Parallel and withdraw them to the North, the French were to do the same and withdraw to the South. It was stipulated that this was a temporary partition until all-Vietnam elections were held in July 1956, to reunify the country. Thus for twenty-one years, there were two separate régimes in North and South Vietnam respectively.

great scholar Nguyen Trai; and finally the peasant, Nguyen Hue. This reflected the situation in which the feudal monarchy was no longer capable of defending the national interest. So it was that in the mid nineteenth century, faced with the danger of losing their country to the French, the peasants rose up everywhere. The feudal Nguyen refused, however, any sort of reforms, and responded by only stepping up their repression, and what was worse, chose to co-operate with the invaders. The people, on the other hand, continued to fight back throughout the century of French occupation, organizing 'troops of the just cause' to wage a resistance.

Vo Nguyen Giap has pointed out[3] that until the time of the French invasion, the national army fought side by side with the regional and local troops, 'the armed forces of the masses', and that this enabled them 'to beat the great with the small, oppose the less numerous to the more numerous, neutralize the long with the short, vanquish the strong with the weak'. He also noted that during their victories against previous invaders, both sides had approximately the same quality of equipment, even though the enemy's effectives were always much greater. The French came with far superior weapons, but Giap – and Nguyen Khac Vien, supported by the majority of other contemporary Vietnamese historians, agrees – believes that the decisive reason for the French success was the supine, capitulationist attitude of the Nguyen dynasty.

There were thirteen important insurrectionary movements between 1861 and 1897, several of them led by noted scholars, all supported by the people of the regions in which they were launched, but none of them on a nationwide scale. Mandarins who had insisted on armed resistance were dismissed. Gia Long, whose reign ended in 1820, had been succeeded by others who pursued the same capitulationist policies, including Tu Duc who died without an heir in July 1883. In a confused period, three kings were enthroned and deposed in as many months because the leading clans and factions in Hue could not agree how to handle the new situation in which the 'guest' originally invited to install the Nguyen dynasty was clearly

3. *Armement des Masses Révolutionnaires, Edification de l' Armée du Peuple*, op cit, pp 79–80.

bent on taking over the whole country. Resist; negotiate the best terms possible; capitulate. These were the three options, and each had its champions in Court circles.

The French – slowed up by the Franco–Prussian War (1870–1) and the Paris Commune (1871) – exploited this dynastic crisis by massing their troops for a drive on Hue, using the threat to pressurize the two regents, Ton Tan Thuyet and Nguyen Van Tong – in charge because of dissent over the choice of king – to ratify an earlier agreement under which Vietnam became a French 'protectorate'. But Ton Tan Thuyet of the pro-resistance faction could not swallow this humiliation, and transferred Court treasures and documents to a hurriedly-built fortress further north in Quang Tri province, near what was to become the North–South dividing line from 1954–75. In July 1884, the twelve-year-old Ham Nghi was enthroned as king, promptly allying himself with the resistance faction. The French, closing in on the capital, demanded the dissolution of the Court army defending Hue, upon which troops under Ton Tan Thuyet attacked French positions. After a fierce battle, they were forced to withdraw and the French occupied Hue. Ton Tan Thuyet and the boy king withdrew to resistance bases in the mountains, where King Ham Nghi issued a famous Proclamation – in many ways similar to that issued by Prince Norodom Sihanouk of Cambodia eighty-five years later – appealing to the people to rally around the monarchy and resist the invaders. He announced the reinstatement of all mandarins dismissed by his predecessors for supporting the resistance. The French riposte was to install a new monarch, King Dong Khanh, in Hue on 19 September 1885.

These momentous events, even at Court level, throughout 1884–5, demonstrate the dogged resistance among all sections of the population to the foreign invasion. It was the more surprising because the French, through the diligent work of the missionaries who had secured the original invasion beachhead, had succeeded in implanting a substantial 'fifth column' of Catholic converts, especially among superstitious fishing communities in the coastal areas, for whose special problems neither Buddhism, Taoism nor Confucianism had provided

78

adequate answers. Catholic assurances, for believers, had a powerful attraction for those so often snatched away by the elements.

The resistance of King Ham Nghi and his followers, supported as it was by the people, was a case of 'too little and too late'. He was captured in November 1888 and at the ripe old age of sixteen was exiled to Algeria, from where he never returned. But his royal Proclamation calmed the consciences of many rebel patriots in the years that followed, torn between their Confucian duty to be loyal to the king and their nationalist sentiments to be loyal to country and people. Armed struggle was particularly strong in the North where the French were on the verge of total defeat on several occasions. They were saved by orders from the Hue Court to resisters to lay down their arms.

An epitaph to the period is the Petition, left by Hoang Dieu, military governor of the Hanoi military temple, on 25 April 1882. He had pleaded in vain for permission to take measures to repel a French attack, preparations for which were building up under his very eyes. His only replies from King Tu Duc were reproaches for advocating an 'inopportune defence'. Hoang Dieu had received his literary doctorate in 1853. The following extract describes the tragic dilemma into which Confucian exigencies of unquestioned loyalty to the sovereign had pushed so many patriots of his day:

I thought that Hanoi, key to the North, was a region vital for the whole country. If it ever collapsed, the other provinces would fall like ripe fruit. Full of anxiety, I launched an urgent appeal to the various regions; I warned the Court. With reinforcements, there was perhaps still time?

Alas. His majesty more than once reproached me for this; accusing me of resorting to pressure of arms and of recommending an inopportune defence. This reprimand seemed to me to be too severe. It was disappointing for the mandarins and the population who didn't know what to do.

Unwilling to trust only my own personal decisions, I none the less had to assume my responsibilities ... Striving at all times to be correct, I followed the example of my ancestors in obeying the cult of the King. I consulted my colleagues daily. Some suggested better open the gates to the enemy. Others that we withdraw our troops to allay suspicions. If my body had to be quartered, my bones ground to powder, I could never subscribe to such measures. While no line of action had yet been decided, the French broke the peace. The seventh day of this month [according to the lunar calendar] they delivered an ultimatum and the following day their soldiers swarmed ahead like ants, their weapons rumbling like thunder. The city streets were ablaze, the citadel lost its combativity. Mastering my misgivings, I rushed to the head of a column. We killed a hundred or so of the enemy and held out for half a day. They were at the peak of their strength – we, exhausted. Without reinforcements we were doomed. Soldiers panicked and ran like rabbits. The civil mandarins at the first news disappeared. I was brokenhearted. What could I do alone? Incapable of commanding, I decided I was unworthy to live ... My death cannot atone for the loss of the citadel ... I have decided however to hang myself to pay my debt as a man, thus following the example of Truong Tan – who died for the citadel.

This decision is not motivated by any pretence of wanting to prove my fidelity and loyalty to my King ...[4]

In October 1964, journalists in Saigon were astounded at the calm and courage of a young electrician, Nguyen Van Troi, who tied to a stake insisted on holding a press conference until the moment that bullets from a firing squad tore into his body. He was executed for having tried to blow up US Secretary of Defence Robert S. McNamara. In denouncing what he considered the Saigon traitor régime and the US military presence literally with his last breath, Nguyen Van Troi was following precedents established a century earlier by patriotic mandarins and scholars, scores of whom left poems

4. *Anthologie de la Littérature Vietnamienne*, op cit, pp 101–2.

burning with patriotism and hatred for the invader before they faced their executioners or took their own lives. But for all their courage and patriotism – the quality of which is inscribed in some of the finest gems of Vietnamese literature – the end was inevitable.

It was a considerable feat of the Vietnamese people, seven million of them at the time of the French invasion in 1858, with no centralized resistance organization, to have held out until 1897, against one of the most experienced European military powers of the day. A significant fact, especially for those who exaggerate the difference in personality and character between North and South Vietnamese, is that the quality of the resistance to the foreign invader then, as a century later, was the same all over the country. Vietnamese heroism and patriotism have never been stopped by Dong Hoi walls or any other temporary demarcation lines.

1 Sampans on the Ma River,
the home country of 'Dame Trieu'

2 The mythical Lac bird, taken from
a bronze drum some three thousand
years old

3 The Trung sisters as depicted in a Hanoi temple built in their honour

4 Tree-trunk stakes
embedded in the Bach
Dang river defeated a
Chinese invasion in 938

5 The temple of the 'Blind Poet'

6 An air-raid warden, with a bronze temple bell for an air-raid siren

7 An unexploded bomb makes a convenient seat for an Vietnamese girl

8 Bringing home the day's bag — the remains of an American Phantom fighter-bomber

9 and 10   Anti-aircraft
defence: village girls in
training

11 Girls being trained in hand-to-hand fighting

12 Bicycles, reinforced with bamboo tubing, could carry up to half a ton of supplies twenty miles a day

13 The most common features at all schools were the trench systems
starting within the classroom . . .

14 . . . and the stretchers for evacuating the wounded

15 Vo Nguyen Giap:
'It was easy'

16 Amid the ruins of the coal
producing city of Hongay,
one hundred per cent destroyed

CHAPTER 8

THE FRENCH CONTRIBUTION

A most convincing confirmation of the quality of the Vietnamese resistance, described in the previous chapter, comes from a French historian, an on-the-spot observer in 1861, at the start of an intense armed struggle in the Saigon–Bien Hoa region. His account would have been equally valid for the Vietminh war against the French, or the Vietcong war against the Americans.[1] The historian, Léopold Pallu, was writing of the area just north of Saigon:

> One would like to put the finger on the main cause for the appearance of these bands which, during the rainy season, seemed to circulate freely around our columns, behind them when they advanced, ahead of them when they returned to their point of departure. They seemed to come up out of the ground. We imagined that there must be some central point from which they fanned out, some point where they had food and other supplies. That is why we concentrated on Bien Hoa. After ·Bien Hoa –

1. The term Vietminh is an abbreviation for the Vietnam Independence League, set up by Ho Chi Minh in 1941, to carry on the resistance war against the French. The Vietcong, was originally a pejorative term invented by the Saigon régime in 1954, to designate anyone opposing the régime. It is an abbreviation for Vietnamese Communists and gradually acquired the prestige of the former Vietminh.

Vinh Long. The fact is that the centre of resistance was everywhere, subdivided *ad infinitum*, almost as many times as there were Annamites. It would be more exact to consider each peasant fastening a sheaf of rice as a resistance centre. The trouble with fighting on a terrain where the enemy can live and hide is that the war becomes personal; it changes its aim and name – and becomes repression.[2]

It was in June 1862 that the Hue Court ceded to France about half the Mekong delta and agreed to pay 20 million francs – an enormous sum for those days – in compensation for French losses in trying to subjugate the country, and gave the French the rights to use the country's three main ports without payment. However, the treaty was not implemented. Local people's forces refused to withdraw from the three ceded provinces. Truong Dinh, their commander, after wrestling with his Confucian conscience, but under strong pressures from the peasant masses, defied the King's orders and, accepting the title 'Commander-in-Chief, Pacifier of the French', he carried on the struggle for two years until he was wounded and committed suicide rather than fall into French hands. It was not until 1867 that the French mustered enough strength to militarily occupy the provinces. The local governor, Phan Thanh Gian, who had negotiated the 1862 treaty under orders from the king, also committed suicide when the provinces were taken over, and it was typical that his son carried on armed resistance.

There was a brief and curious interlude during the French invasion in which King Tu Duc appealed to Peking for help, and the Ch'ings politely sent a token 10,000 troops into the northern provinces, stopping well short of Hanoi. After their experiences with the Tay Son, however, the Ch'ings had no interest in burning their fingers again in trying to pull 'chestnuts out of the fire' to save the Nguyens. They were glad to sign a treaty with France (May 1884), and following two clashes with French troops in the Lang Son pass which was

2. Léopold Pallu, *Histoire de l'Expedition de Cochinchine en 1861* (Paris, 1864).

promptly followed by two French retaliatory attacks on China, a second treaty was signed (June 1885), under which China totally renounced its rights in Vietnam. Once the French considered they had consolidated their military takeover, they started eliminating Chinese cultural influence – as the Americans were later to try to eliminate the French cultural influence – both copying the earlier Chinese example of trying to liquidate Vietnam's own culture. The education system was one of the early targets and particularly the use of Chinese characters. Huynh Khac Dung, the poet and specialist on the traditional Vietnamese educational system, mentioned in Chapter 6, has some pertinent remarks to make on the French effort in his essays *L'Enseignement dans l'Ancien Vietnam* (Saigon, 1952).

For political reasons, France tried several times to re-place this [Vietnamese] system by another. At first it was the missionaries who, having preceded the administrators, tried from the moment of their arrival, to find a con-venient means of expanding the propagation of their ideas. It was the Reverend Father Alexandre de Rhodes who had the merit of latinizing the Vietnamese language, thus enabling it to more rapidly reach the broad masses of believers. This innovation, which the first administra-tors did not fail to exploit for their colonial policies, created in a way the first bases for a vigorous struggle against the moral system to which the educational system of the Vietnamese people was closely linked.

Although liberal and tolerant in regard to religions, the Confucian system was of deep secular inspiration. By the very fact of its high prestige, by the strictness and precision of its precepts, by its positive character and absence of any mysticism, it had always won out in resisting the expansion of Christianity. It was therefore considered necessary to strongly attack this ancient culture, of which the representatives in Vietnam had been the most resolute enemies of the triumphant French. It was necessary to give to our people the means of freeing itself from the Chinese yoke on the cultural front.

85

In South Vietnam, by the creation of French schools in which the French language and *quoc ngu*[3] were taught at the same time, the French – with the stroke of a pen – suppressed the old educational system. This Draconian measure so upset public opinion that the Vietnamese tried to evade an obligation which they considered unpleasant – to say the least! To recruit pupils the French at times had to resort to force. Every village had to supply a defined quota of children, which caused great dismay among the families. To spare their children the penance of going to French schools, there were parents who paid buffalo-boys to go in their place. Naturally the results hoped for were far from being attained. Pupils thus trained by makeshift teachers, without any pedagogical qualifications, were so inadequate that the propagation of the French language was greatly hampered.

Although Huynh Khac Dung does not specifically say so, a high degree of illiteracy started to manifest itself in Vietnam from this period and continued until – during the wars against the French and Americans – liberated areas were set up by the Vietnamese where education in their own language, as expressed in *quoc ngu*, and anti-illiteracy campaigns were launched. Whether the buffalo-boys, usually from the poorest of the poor village families, derived any benefit from this, Huynh Khac Dung does not say. One buffalo-boy did benefit, however, and that was the father of Ho Chi Minh! (The hiring of such surrogates was repeated a century later when the wealthy hired sons of the poor to replace their own in the ranks of the Saigon Army!)

The system of forced attendance at French language schools in Cochin-Chine was a failure and in Annam and Tonking the French, for a time, maintained the traditional system, but with teaching in French and Vietnamese. According to

3. *Quoc ngu*, or national language, was the latinized version of spoken Vietnamese invented by the Reverend Father Alexandre de Rhodes to oust the *nom* which had been made the official language for education by King Quang Trung in the eighteenth century, but had been used by such noted poets as Nguyen Trai three centuries earlier. The French aimed to introduce French as the sole national language!

Huynh Khac Dung this did not work either. 'It was a fiasco. It produced nincompoops as administrators; individuals infatuated with themselves but shabby caricatures of scholars who dashed the hopes of the French administration to the ultimate degree.'[4]

However, the system of examinations by elimination continued in Annam and Tonking to produce 'bachelors' and 'masters' culminating in the triennial exams at which the precious 'doctor' degrees were awarded. But some of the graduates poured poetic scorn on the French modifications of their classical system. For the triennial competitions of 1897, rumours spread that Governor-General Paul Doumer was going to impose *quoc ngu* as the script for the literary contests. A noted satirist, Tran Te Xuong, hastened to comment:

> Rumour has it that from now on scholarship will have another face.
> Let our scholars hasten for this last contest!
> But even if they suppress the stelae in stone,
> A thousand years will not suffice to suppress those of the mouth.
> Gentlemen! Throw away your brushes and take their pencils![5]

Huynh Khac Dung in his book maintains that although there was some merit in the introduction of *quoc ngu* as the language of instruction at all levels, as well as the study of western science, the changes of the existing educational system did not produce the results hoped for by the French. He goes on to point out that graduates from this system finished with very poor qualifications, indeed, they were poor representa-

4. *L'Enseignement dans l'Ancien Vietnam*, op cit.
5. *Anthologie de la Littérature Vietnamienne*, op cit, p 169. Tran Te Xuong was obviously suggesting that just as the Chinese ideographs, painted with brush, had served to express spoken Vietnamese, the pencil to write a latinized version should be used for the same purpose. He also suggests that the practice of engraving the names of successful candidates on stone stelae at Hanoi's Temple of Literature was to be abolished by the French – as it was.

tives of both French and Vietnamese cultures. Faced with such a situation, the French had either to retreat or energetically go ahead with radical measures. Thus, France abolished the triennial competitions, for Vietnam apparently a *coup de grace* for written Chinese, and instituted a university together with higher schools of law and administration, of science, medicine and pharmaceutics. Clearly this modern educational system opened up a new era in the field of Vietnamese culture, and ideas rapidly developed in favour of western thinking, at the same time as the prestige of Chinese learning declined.

But there did remain, according to Huynh Khac Dung, an old background of Far-Eastern civilization, based on the Five Cardinal Virtues: *Nhan*, love for humanity; *Nghia*, justice; *Le*, courtesy, in accordance with established rituals; *Tri*, wisdom and prudence; and *Tin*, loyalty and confidence. Moreover, he points out that a profound difference of mentality which existed between the French and Vietnamese constituted a serious obstacle to a perfect assimilation of the lessons from the new master. As an avowed Confucian, Huynh Khac Dung recognized in his writing that suppression of the old educational system had resulted in the weakening of the Confucian concept of duty, and was replaced by an ever-growing individualism avid, in his own words, 'for riches and comforts'.

The evaluation of the educational system introduced by the French as expressed by the Confucian, Huynh Khac Dung, is not different from that expressed by the Marxist, Nguyen Khac Vien, although they were writing from Saigon and Hanoi respectively, with Nguyen Khac Vien writing ten years later.

At all levels it was a third-rate education. Even the Indo-chinese University, opened in 1908, dispensed a truncated and deformed education. French was the teaching medium, the study of the national language and history was reduced to a minimum. School and college students learnt by heart that 'our ancestors were the Gauls' and discoursed all day long on Racine or Chateaubriand without ever seriously tackling the study of Vietnamese culture. Even French authors of the eighteenth century such as Montesquieu and Rousseau were prohibited; there was neither a faculty of sciences nor an engineering school at the Indochinese University. The main feature of colonial education was its restricted character. The diffusion of instruction was restricted to the utmost. In traditional Vietnam, despite all the hindrances of the feudal régime, the population who craved for instruction managed to set up classes for children in almost every village. The substitution of the colonial education for the traditional one provoked a sharp decrease in the number of schools and pupils; an extension of illiteracy.

One of the most pressing demands of the Vietnamese people during the colonial period was the diffusion and the Vietnamization of education. Under this constant pressure the colonial administration was compelled to set up a few educational establishments.

The University created in 1908 was mainly meant to keep in the country the youths who wanted to go and study in Japan. But never was there any important diffusion of education. Ninety per cent of the children could not go to school. There were never more than three secondary schools for the whole of Vietnam (the same number as for the children of the French who totalled only a few score thousand). Thirty years after its founding, the University had an enrolment of only 600 students.[6]

It is an extraordinary fact, unknown to the outside world, except for a few specialists, that far from bringing enlightenment and education and what was positive in western civilization to Vietnam, French colonialism actually destroyed a system which, with occasional modifications, existed from

6. *Vietnam: A Short Historical Sketch*, op cit, pp 166–7. The interest in studying in Japan was enormously stimulated by the Japanese victory in the Russo–Japanese War (1904–5). The notion that an Asiatic country could defeat a great western power had an obvious fascination for young Vietnamese patriots, 200 of whom – mostly sons of scholar-resistants – were in Japan by 1908.

1075 to 1908; turning a highly literate people into a nation of illiterates.

If the French impact on education and culture in general was disastrous, their exactions in the economic sphere were equally unsatisfactory. The French had to rely from the beginning upon the most reactionary class, the rapacious landlords among the Vietnamese, the feudal chiefs of the mountain tribespeople, strengthening their powers and privileges as a reward for their loyalties. As the resistance came from the peasantry and the scholars, it was logical that the French should make a tacit alliance with the worst enemies of the peasants and scholars, starting, of course, with the Nguyen dynasty. Accordingly, they took the best of the land for their rice, coffee and rubber plantations, and by the eve of World War I, they had expropriated 470,000 hectares, 306,000 of them in the rice-rich Mekong delta, the rest for coffee and rubber plantations in the Central Highlands. Another 90,000 hectares of forest – including teak and other valuable hardwoods – were also taken over. Vietnam, too, became a comfortable resort for all sorts of place-seekers and bureaucrats who could not quite make the grade in France, or who had special 'protection' in political circles. But the number of French civilian functionaries was excessive by any standards. Indeed, it was 5,000 by 1910, which was approximately the number the British had in India at that time with about fifty times the population. And it was the Vietnamese people who had to pay for it all, as well as the salary of every soldier and the price of every bullet fired in suppressing their resistance; the costs of building everything from the palaces of the governors to the jails of the resisters.

Everything, therefore, that was retrograde and reactionary in the old régime, from the system of unpaid forced labour to the landlords' power of life and death over the peasants and those of seigneurs, sorcerers and witch-doctors over the ethnic minorities, was maintained and strengthened in the name of 'preserving local customs'. But innumerable new forms of taxes were introduced, including head taxes and land taxes which doubled, trebled or quadrupled from year to year, according to French needs. Not only were local needs satisfied, but those of metropolitan France, too! The most in-famous – and profitable – form of tax-collecting was the excise duty on alcohol, opium and salt, the French having established a monopoly on these three products. One might think that the Vietnamese had only to refrain from drinking alcohol and smoking opium, and two-thirds of these excise taxes would not apply. It was not so simple, however.

Salt was obviously an essential and check-points were set up all over the country to collect the taxes in case non-government salt was moved from the coastal areas to the interior. The resulting large increase in the price of salt (five-fold between 1889 and 1907) seriously affected the health of the mountain peoples, the incidence of goitres sharply increasing due to the lack of iodine – which is normally in-gested with the sea salt. The French forced opium on the Vietnamese in the same way that the British had forced it on the Chinese twenty or so years earlier. The import concession was originally granted to two Frenchmen, who quickly made a fortune, but after scandals connected with their smuggling in large quantities of the drug in excess of the official quota, the traffic temporarily passed into the hands of Cholon Chinese. But at the beginning of the twentieth century, the French exercised an absolute monopoly in growing the poppy, transforming it into opium and selling it on the local or export markets. In one form or another, official, semi-official, or clandestine, the French administration drew enormous profits from the opium traffic and encouraged opium smoking to the maximum.

The most scandalous of the taxes was probably that con-cerning alcohol. Each village was forced to purchase a mini-mum quota of litres per head of the population according to the number of inhabitants. The monopoly on the manufacture, importation and sale of alcohol having been granted to the French firm of Fontaine in 1902, the French administration could thus calculate with absolute precision its minimum an-nual revenue from the per capita consumption, or at least purchase, of alcohol. When I travelled through the villages of North Vietnam for the first time, in early 1954, the taxes on salt and alcohol, and the harsh controls associated with their enforcement, were the subject of some of the bitterest criticisms of the French that I was to hear from the peasants. In the plains, as in the mountain areas, the peasants traditionally brew a vodka-type alcohol from rice, generally known as 'shum-shum', but under the French private brewing was forbidden. The minimum punishment was prison, but it could also result in confiscation of property or even deportation. The firm of Fontaine was reputed to receive an annual 80 to 90 per cent return on its invested capital, and the price of alcohol jumped 500 per cent within the first few years of the operations.

It seems evident that, while bearing the burdens of the French régime, the peasants received little benefit; they were too poor to buy French industrial goods and no one taught them the new agricultural techniques which would improve production. And it could be argued that the administration was more concerned with building railways and roads of strategic importance than with constructing hydraulic works to protect the crops from natural calamities. In fact, under the French system, per capita rice consumption decreased from 262 kgs in 1900 to 226 kgs in 1913.

At the end of the nineteenth century France, from its base in Indochina, and the British, based in Burma, were competing to push into China through the back door of Yunnan province, both Vietnam and Burma having common frontiers with that province. The French won, by building a 530 kms railway through the formidable mountain chain which forms the Vietnam–China border to link Hanoi with the Yunnan provincial capital of Kunming, securing special economic privileges there. Ninety thousand Vietnamese peasants were conscripted to do the muscle work, 25,000 of whom died. The railway was completed in 1910.

The infinite capacity for hard work of the Vietnamese peasantry and their considerable abilities as soldiers – proven by resistance to the French – was not overlooked as the war clouds gathered in Europe for World War I. To support France's quarrels with the Germany of Kaiser Wilhelm – in which the stake was the carving up of Germany's colonial empire – 99,000 Vietnamese peasants were plucked from the warm mud of their ricefields and implanted in the harsh and inhospitable mud of Flanders and other French battlefields. Fifty thousand were conscripted as combat troops, the others as coolies to dig trenches in Verdun and carry shells.

Two years before the outbreak of World War I, a young villager whose name at birth was Nguyen Sinh Cung, but who was renamed at the age of ten, in accordance with Vietnamese tradition, Nguyen Tat Thanh, enlisted on the French windjammer, *Latouche Tréville*, as a cook's assistant. Under the name of 'Ba', he set forth from Saigon to see the world and understand it. Among a dozen other names he was to adopt in the half century that followed, it was that of Ho Chi Minh (meaning Ho the Enlightened One) that finally stuck, with Nguyen Ai Quoc (Nguyen the Patriot) coming a close second.

Ho Chi Minh turned out to be the hero for which the situation was searching. Nothing that makes any sense can be written about today's Vietnam without understanding what went into the making of Ho Chi Minh and what he did to make Vietnam and the Vietnamese what they are today. 'Uncle Ho' represented the synthesis of the great patriots in his country's age-old history. His impact was so great that it is no exaggeration to state that the secret of the globe-shaking events in Vietnam during March/April 1975, was that he managed to inject something of himself into every contemporary Vietnamese revolutionary.

CHAPTER 9

ENTER 'UNCLE HO'

Ho Chi Minh's father, Nguyen Sinh Sac, was the perfect example of the peasant scholar-patriot, who rejected the honours and privileges of court life, to remain close to his people. His native village of Kim Lien in Nghe An province (north-central Vietnam), was locally known as *Lang Dai Kho* (Loincloth village) because of its poverty. But it was also in the home district of the great poet, Nguyen Du, and a temple close to Kim Lien was dedicated to the fifteenth-century guerilla hero, Le Loi, who had expelled the Ming invaders. It was in Nghe An and the neighbouring province of Thanh Hoa that Nguyen had raised his first 50,000 troops to throw out the Ch'ings. Nguyen Sinh Sac's uncle, Hoang Xuan Hanh, had fought with a noted resistance leader, De Tham, who had held out against the French for thirty years. Captured by the French and while trussed up awaiting torture and interrogation, Hoang Xuan Hanh had banged his jaw against the ground to bite off half his tongue to avoid risking betraying secrets under torture.

Born of a concubine and starting life as a buffalo-boy, Nguyen Sinh Sac, by dint of hard study was able to shed these social handicaps. He proved to be an outstanding scholar and worked his way up to compete in the 1900 triennial examinations to win a doctorship (second class). Symbolic of the popular veneration of literary honours, the local population wanted to prepare a triumphal welcome for the new doctor. Deciding that his tiny hut was unworthy of his new status, they contributed money to buy him a five-room house with a piece of land to mark the fame his scholarship had bestowed on Kim Lien.

Automatically qualifying as a mandarin, Dr Nguyen Sinh Sac was quickly disgusted by the corruption and privileges of court life, the gap between the misery of the peasantry and the luxury at Hue. He returned to teach in his village, to supervise the education of Nguyen Tat Thanh, who quickly showed promise of becoming a brilliant pupil. At the age of fifty, the famous scholar learned French, and then left his village to wander through the countryside as an itinerant story-teller, letter-writer and an occasional dispenser of traditional medicines, a kindly, gentle man to the last, according to accounts of those who met him during his wanderings. It was impossible for young Tat Thanh not to be influenced by the atmosphere in which he grew up, including the family legend of his great-uncle's patriotism, his father's renunciation of the honours of a mandarin's status, the temples and legendary tales of local heroes who had contributed so much to Vietnamese history.

Two events left a particular impression on the young man. On 14 July 1901, a prestigious scholar-patriot, Dr (first class) Phan Boi Chau, close friend of Nguyen Sinh Sac and a boyhood hero of Tat Thanh, led an attack on the French citadel in the Nghe An provincial capital. It failed, but marked the start of a long resistance campaign headed by Phan Boi Chau. He later went to Japan in the vain belief that the régime which had defeated Tsarist Russia would help Vietnamese patriots to remove the French. Later he tried to persuade Tat Thanh and his brother to join a group of young people he was taking back to Japan for training as revolutionaries. They refused, despite the tremendous admiration the fifteen-year-old Tat Thanh had for the poetry and patriotism of Phan Boi Chau. Why the refusal? According to Ho Chi Minh's biographers, Hoai Thanh and Thanh Tinh:

He vaguely realized that there was something not quite

right in this campaign which attempted to win over local mandarins to rekindle the flame of a movement in support of the throne, which had a prince as its device and Japan as its main support. The prospect of studying in the land of the Mikado left him cold.[1]

Teenager Nguyen Tat Thanh listened in to the many conversations his father had with Phan Boi Chau, not only regarding the poet-patriot's own plans, but also their discussions on the ups and downs of various other resistance movements. The second important influence in his youth was the continual French manpower raids – often at night – in search of 'coolies' for their road- and rail-building projects. Being conscripted for such work in the malaria-ridden forests along the Vietnam–Laos border was almost the equivalent of a death warrant. All males between eighteen and fifty were obliged to register for corvée and, although the family of Nguyen Sinh Sac was exempt because of his rank of mandarin, he was so moved by the sufferings of those being marched off to the mines or work projects that at one period Nguyen Sinh Sac sold his ricefields – given with the house by villagers – and distributed the money, as long as it lasted, to those being dragged off for forced labour service. The suffering of the peasantry, the humiliation of living under foreign overlords, his father's deep humanity, the conspiratorial conversations with patriots like Phan Boi Chau – such were some of the factors that left indelible impressions and helped to forge the resolve to grasp the torch of revolt from the hands of his elders.

Nguyen Tat Thanh started studying at the French-run Quoc Hoc college at Hue, after a thorough grounding in the Chinese classics from his father and another noted teacher,

1. Hoi Thanh and Thanh Tinh (eds), *Souvenirs sur Ho Chi Minh* (Hanoi, 1965), p 29. Phan Boi Chau had formed the *Dong Du* (Go East) student movement, in his enthusiasm for Japanese education, also the *Quang Phuc Hoi* (Association for the Restoration of Vietnam), which advocated assassinating leading French and puppet officials. He had also won over Prince Cuong De, of the Nguyen dynasty, whom he hoped would lead a more enlightened monarchy. Cuong De was among the 200 young patriots whom Phan Boi Chau had persuaded by 1908 to go to Japan. It was this 'brain drain' for obviously revolutionary purposes which frightened the French into opening a university in Hanoi in 1908.

Hoang Phan Quynh. However, he immediately realized that the only aim of French education was to train students to help the French in their exploitation of the Vietnamese people, so he left to teach in a private school for a short time. After this, Nguyen Tat Thanh went to Saigon to learn something about seafaring in a French-organized technical school. At the age of twenty he had already made up his mind to go abroad and pick up what knowledge he could to further the aims of the independence struggle. (One of his fellow students at the technical school was a certain Ton Duc Thang, who later entered history by shinning up the mast of the flagship of the French Black Sea Fleet and unfurling the red flag of mutiny. The sailors had decided against taking part in a French attempt to put down the Bolshevik revolution and while they were locking up their officers in the hold, the young Vietnamese was signalling the word to the rest of the fleet. The result was that the fleet had to put about and return to Toulon. When Ho Chi Minh died in 1969, it was Ton Duc Thang who succeeded him as President, and still another veteran sailor, Nguyen Luong Bang, who took over from Ton Duc Thang as Vice-President.)

The young Ho, as we may now call him, although he used the name 'Ba' at that time, broke off a three-year course after three months and managed, with the aptitude he had, to sign on the French steamer, *Admiral Latouche Tréville*, as a cook's helper. Once in France, he found a job as a servant to a French family in Le Havre, then took to sea again, visiting a great number of French colonies as well as the United States.

Two main impressions, he was later to tell me, resulted from his first contacts with the outside world. The first was that colonialist exploitation was the same everywhere. 'To the colonialists, the life of an Asian is not worth a cent,' he commented. He then went on to relate an incident which had obviously occupied a special place in his memory because he referred to it on several occasions. He had seen four Africans drown, one after another as they tried to swim a line ashore during a terrible storm off Dakar, the port and capital of Senegal. 'The French treated it as a joke,' he said. 'The officers stood around laughing while the Africans died for their sake.' The second impression was that the French he met as shipmates or in the cafés and homes in Marseilles, Le Havre and other ports, were very different from the colonialists he had encountered in Vietnam. The ordinary French are 'good' he concluded, once he got to know them at home and at work.

The early distinction between colonialists and French people, the complete absence of any racial hatred towards the French and the observations of an exceptionally sensitive, alert mind during his travels, laid the basis for the breadth and depth of Ho Chi Minh's international outlook which he preserved to the day of his death and which he encouraged generations of Vietnamese to copy. Notes made during those travels were to serve him well later when he plunged into journalism and writing. His first book, typically enough, was entitled *Le Procès de la Colonialisation Français* (Accusations against French Colonialism), published by Librairie de Travail in Paris in 1925.

After his sea travels were over, Ho went to London in the winter of 1913, doing any odd jobs he could pick up, sweeping snow, working as a boiler tender in a lodging-house basement. Among other extraordinary adventures was that of working as an assistant to Escoffier, still considered by the French as their greatest chef, at London's Carlton Hotel. As a dish-washer, he had come to the great man's attention when he heard that the frugal Oriental had the habit of trimming half-eaten steaks and either sending them back to the kitchen, or wrapping them in paper and leaving them at night near the garbage cans where the hungry came to scavenge. Sending for the young man, Escoffier asked what this was all about. 'Good food shouldn't be thrown away', replied the unabashed dish-washer. 'It should be given to the poor.' There followed a conversation in Escoffier's native French. Something must have attracted him to young 'Ba', as he was still known, because the upshot was that Escoffier laughed and said: 'Forget your revolutionary ideas. I'll teach you to cook instead. Then you'll become rich and famous.' So the future president was promoted to the cake-making department!

In his spare time – his study a bench in Hyde Park for use

99

in off-duty hours – he learned English. He also studied the history of the struggles of Asian and African people in the English, as well as the French, Portuguese and Dutch colonies. But the question of how to win his own country's independence was always uppermost in his mind. And the conscripting of Vietnamese as 'coolies' and cheap cannon fodder for European battlefields fanned the embers of his determination to act. His first chance came when the major powers gathered at Versailles for the great conference that followed Germany's defeat in World War I. Ho had returned to France in 1917, contacting other Vietnamese there who shared his views. There was great excitement among the Vietnamese community in Paris when in June 1919, Nguyen Ai Quoc presented a petition to the Versailles Conference. It was a document simple and to the point, as was the Testament he wrote just fifty years later when he knew his days were numbered. A sworn enemy of clichés and jargon and with a sense of frugality in all things – including language – his spoken and written words were usually models of clarity. The points included in the petition were as follows:

1. General amnesty for all Vietnamese political prisoners.
2. Equal rights for Vietnamese and French in Indochina, suppression of the Criminal Commissions which are instruments of terrorism aimed at Vietnamese patriots.
3. Freedom of press and opinion.
4. Freedom to travel at home and abroad.
5. Freedom to study, and the opening of technical and professional schools for natives of the colonies. [At that time the French ruled Indochina as a single bloc, but with different status – colonies and protectorates – for the five components which included Laos and Cambodia as well as the three Vietnamese subdivisions of Cochin-Chine, Annam and Tonking.]
6. Substitute the rule of law for government by decree.
7. Appointment of a Vietnamese delegation alongside that of the French government to settle questions relating to Vietnamese interests.

As in all his subsequent dealings with France, Ho Chi Minh's demands were modest. He was not even asking the French to abandon their colonial régime in Indochina, only to introduce some minimal reforms to ease the immediate conditions of his compatriots and to restore some semblance of national dignity. France turned a deaf ear to his demands, but Nguyen 'The Patriot' had succeeded in attracting publicity in French progressive circles. Indeed, from that time on he had a public and journalistic outlet through which to make his voice heard.

The rejection by the French government reinforced his views that revolutionary struggle was the only way, and he started organizing for this with the singleness of purpose that marked his entire life. He joined the French Socialist Party, the first Vietnamese to be admitted as a member of any political party. Through its organs he exposed the conditions of the colonized in Vietnam and other countries. He founded a newspaper, *La Paria*, editing it with North African expatriates and distributing it throughout the colonies using his old seafaring connections. It was typical that he was able to turn to good account each of his accumulated experiences to further the cause, not only of Vietnam, but of all colonial peoples.

At the famous Tours Congress (25–30 December 1920), at which the French Socialist Party split in two over whether to adhere to the Second or Third (Communist) International, Nguyen Ai Quoc, a full delegate, voted for the Third International because it had taken a firm anti-colonial position. He thus became the first Vietnamese Communist and a founding member of the French Communist Party which was born out of the split. From then on, he was on an organized road, but it is important to note that his option for the Second and Third International had nothing to do with ideological abstractions, but was based on one very practical issue – which side came down more weightily in favour of independence for the colonies. Later he was to criticize with some severity the vacillating attitudes at various periods of the French and British Communist Parties on the colonial question. He was, above all, a patriot in search of a foolproof line leading to the recovery of Vietnam's independence but not, as in the old days, independence in the hands of a feudal and exploiting ruling class. No more dynasties – power in the hands of those that had always fought hardest for it, those who grew the rice and caught the fish. This concept represented a watershed in the age-old struggles of the Vietnamese people to have their destinies in their own hands. From the Hung kings to Phan Boi Chau, through legend, history and reality, the search had always been for the 'good' king to replace the 'bad' or incompetent one, incapable of leading the people through the dangers that threatened their national existence. Commoners and peasants like Le Loi and Nguyen Hue had built new dynasties on the foundations of their victories. Even Phan Boi Chau dreamed of enthroning a new, enlightened monarch.

It was Nguyen Ai Quoc who launched the concept of the people as sovereign; of a new People's dynasty, in which the dynamics of change would finally project the people (essentially the peasantry) up the spiral of power. There is no question that this is what fascinated him about the Bolshevik revolution, and was the reason why he went to the Soviet Union to have a long look at what could be useful in that revolution, could serve the aim which dominated all his thinking – how to make Vietnam free and keep it free.

Was the Bolshevik revolution a suitable model for Vietnam? Ho Chi Minh had a good look and decided it was not. Tsarist Russia, although backward industrially compared with Britain, France or Germany, had an industrial working class. Less numerous than the peasantry they were none the less an organized progressive force in the cities. So power was first seized in the cities and then gradually it had to be enforced in the countryside, often against a reluctant peasantry, opposed to change, especially when force was employed to secure that change. Apart from a few illustrious examples, Tolstoy amongst them, intellectuals had gradually sunk their roots into the cities.

In Vietnam, however, it was different. The industrial working class was very weak, mainly restricted to building or maintaining roads and railways, mining and a few textile plants. The peasants had proved themselves to be a revolu-

102

tionary force throughout the ages and the intellectuals – the custodians of culture and traditions – had to a great extent not pulled up their roots from the soil. This accounted for a cohesion and strength in rural society not matched in the urban centres where both the working class and capitalist class were comparatively weak and inexperienced.

From the Soviet Union, at the end of 1924, Ho Chi Minh went to Canton in China, as a secretary to Mikhail Borodin, the Soviet head of a Comintern[2] aid mission to the Kuomintang, then headed by Sun Yat Sen. Ho Chi Minh accepted the assignment, not only to make his contribution to the Chinese revolution – as the staunch internationalist that he was – but to see what he could learn, and organize, to speed up the process in his own country. There is also good reason to think that Ho's decision to arrange a transfer to Canton was spurred on by the explosion of a bomb hurled at the French Governor-General of Indochina, Merlin, as he passed through Canton. Merlin escaped, and the Vietnamese, Pham Hong Thai, committed suicide by throwing himself into the Pearl river.

As it has been demonstrated time and again, heroism and self-sacrifice were never lacking in Vietnam, but were even successful assassinations justified? It was a question with which Ho had to grapple, especially as he moved closer to the scene. Part of his special quality was to react quickly to new situations; seize the essential and see how it could be turned to advantage. Pham Hong Thai belonged to a China-based group, the *Tam Tam Xa* (Union of Hearts), one of many fragmented organizations which were all united in one thing – determination to get rid of the French. Its members believed in individual terrorism which Ho knew in his heart was hopeless. But here were patriots, ready to sacrifice themselves to liberate the country. For a leader in search of a movement, here was a starting point. But here was also a tendency which should be checked before it got out of hand and precious

2. The Comintern, or Communist (Third) International, was set up in Moscow in March 1919, to co-ordinate activities of Communist parties throughout the world. It was dissolved in May 1943, and partially replaced by the Cominform (Communist Information Agency) which in turn was dissolved in April 1956.

human material wasted in vain effort. Too much had already been thrown away in actions doomed to failure. Whatever the deeper motive, Ho Chi Minh, using the name of Vuong Son Nhi, arrived in Canton shortly after the attempt on Governor Merlin, but his strict discipline of secrecy, plus his modesty as to his own role in the revolution, makes it difficult to decide whether the timing was connected with the start of the individual terrorist tactics.

Within six months, Vuong Son Nhi had persuaded the members of the *Tam Tam Xa* to renounce their tactics of individual assassinations and transform themselves into the Revolutionary Youth Association. A few years later, they became part of the Communist Party of Indochina, set up in Portuguese Macao in 1930.

How could Ho Chi Minh persuade people of very different views to his own to accept his pattern for victory? It was an astonishing constant of his leadership. There was nothing obviously imposing about him; no declamations or oratory. Bui Lam, a seafaring compatriot of Ho Chi Minh, and later a member of the Vietnamese Communist Party's General Committee, relates that in July 1922, having finally arrived at the right address, at 6 rue des Gobelins in Paris 13, he knocked on the door:

I heard some steps approaching, the door opened. A man of about thirty to thirty-two, slender, even thin, with a light complexion stood before me, smiling:
'Who do you want?' (I was very young then, less than twenty years.)
'I am looking for Monsieur Nguyen Ai Quoc.'
'That's me! Come in!'
So, I was face to face with Nguyen Ai Quoc! It was he who was smiling in such a friendly way now, opening wide the door! I remember remaining a few seconds without moving, attentively looking to see if the man who came to open and the one who introduced himself were the same. No possible doubt, the same slight build, same threadbare suit of black cloth and, above all, those eyes, those astonishingly shining eyes. I followed him into his

104

room, feeling immediately at ease with not the slightest embarrassment.[3]

Nothing could more accurately describe my own impression on meeting Ho Chi Minh for the first time – in March 1954, at his headquarters, deep in the jungle of Tay Nguyen in the northern part of North Vietnam. I had travelled five days by train from Peking to a spot near the border, then in the back of a truck by night and finally by horse-back to a small clearing, where there were some thatch-roofed huts protected from spy planes by the natural cover of dense jungle. A thick mat of branches from jungle giants met high over the tops of the huts to blot out the sky.

A wind-breaker jacket worn cape-like over his shoulders, a white pith sun-helmet on his head, walking briskly with the aid of a bamboo stick – there he was: Ho Chi Minh. The unmistakable avuncular face, the twinkling, depthless black eyes, above all, the thin wispy beard, a face known from photographs and portraits for years past! At that time the French had announced his death so often that no one knew for sure that he was alive. In fluent English, he enquired about my health, how I had stood up to the journey. After some preliminary exchanges I asked why the French radio in Hanoi was making so much noise about a place called Dien Bien Phu.

'This is Dien Bien Phu,' he said, and tipped his sun-helmet upside down on the table. 'Here are the mountains,' and his slim, strong fingers traced the outside rim of the helmet, 'and that's where we are. Down here,' and his fist plunged to the bottom of the helmet, 'this is the valley of Dien Bien Phu. There are the French. They can't get out.' It was the picture that remained in my mind some weeks later at the opening of the Geneva Conference on 7 May 1954.[4]

Simplicity, sincerity, frankness were part of the strength of

3. *Souvenirs sur Ho Chi Minh*, op cit, pp 48–9.

4. With superb timing, after fifty-five days and nights of bitter fighting, the Vietminh forces won the battle of Dien Bien Phu on the very day the Conference opened. Over 16,000 élite troops of the French Expeditionary Corps were wiped out or surrendered. This defeat was decisive in bringing the French to sign the Geneva Agreement and end the war.

his personal appeal to all who met him. Everybody mentioned his eyes. 'Thin, but strong with very bright eyes', wrote Nguyen Luong Bang, now Vice-President of the Socialist Republic of Vietnam, of his first meeting with 'Vuong Son Nhi' in Canton. 'His gentle voice and cordial manner attracted me at once.'⁵ After a couple of such meetings Nguyen Luong Bang volunteered for the dangerous task of returning to Vietnam to carry on organizational work there. 'The life of President Ho Chi Minh has the purity of light', was how Pham Van Dong, one of his early recruits in Canton, was later to sum up his own assessment of the man who so influenced his own life.

'Uncle Ho' was able to gather around him revolutionaries of extraordinary quality ready for any sacrifice because he was able to infuse them with the same singleness of purpose as his own. This was spelt out in a simple message to the Vietnamese people when he returned after thirty years of exile: 'I have had only one aim in life: to struggle for the good of the country and the well-being of my people. It is for this reason that I have had to hide in the mountains, crouch in prisons. Whatever the moment, wherever the place, I have had a single aim, the interest of the nation, the good of the people.'⁶

This was expressed again when he knew that the last chapter in his life was at hand, and he wrote in his Testament: 'About personal matters – all my life I have served the Fatherland, the revolution and the people with all my heart and strength. If I should now depart from this world, I would have nothing to regret, except not being able to serve longer and more.'

From his activities in Canton, and from the pamphlets and articles smuggled in, word spread that the legendary Nguyen Ai Quoc was there. Thus Canton became a Mecca for ardent young revolutionaries seeking the right way and the right leader. Among them was a mandarin's son, Pham Van Dong. He was later to tell me that in the mid 1920s students like himself were stirred by two important events. One was the arrest – in the French concession of Shanghai – of Phan Boi

5. *Souvenirs sur Ho Chi Minh,* op cit, p 63.

6. Wilfred Burchett, *Ho Chi Minh: An Appreciation* (The Guardian, New York, 1972), p 27.

Chau who, after disillusionment in Japan, had gone to China after the Sun Yat Sen revolution had overthrown the Manchus. His arrest provoked widespread student demonstrations. The other was the death in 1926, in Saigon, of another great scholar-patriot, Phan Chu Trinh who, unlike Phan Boi Chau, had fought for the abolition of the monarchy and the mandarin system. However, the students were not allowed to take part in the funeral ceremonies, and because of this went on strike. It was at this time that Pham Van Dong heard that Nguyen Ai Quoc, whose name was known through articles under his signature, had started a centre for training revolutionary cadres. Thus, taking advantage of the strike, he got in touch with a secret revolutionary organization, and it was arranged that he should leave for Canton. Once there, Pham Van Dong became a member of the League of Revolutionary Vietnamese Youth which Nguyen Ai Quoc had set up. Among the studies Pham Van Dong undertook in Canton was a course at the famous Whampoa Military Academy, where Chiang Kai-shek was chief military instructor. Chou En-lai was in charge of political education and Mikhail Borodin, assisted by Nguyen Ai Quoc, represented the Comintern.

By April 1927, when Chiang Kai-shek started massacring his Communist allies in Shanghai and Canton and members of the Borodin mission had to flee for their lives, 'Uncle Ho' had trained and returned over two hundred cadres – including Pham Van Dong – to Vietnam.

Another phase had come to an end. The Youth Association transferred its headquarters to Hong Kong; Vuong Son Nhi, after a brief underground visit to Shanghai, went on to Moscow; and Pham Van Dong and the 'first two hundred' started their conspiratorial work inside Vietnam. By the time Chiang Kai-shek had crushed the Canton Commune and, as a by-product, had dispersed the leadership-in-exile of the Vietnamese revolution, an irreversible process had been set in motion. It was going to take many years of difficult organizational work; of political struggle and education of Vietnam's peasants and workers. Indeed it was to be nearly twenty years before the first shots were fired. Anyone who thinks that armed struggle is something to be undertaken lightly should ponder

107

over the Vietnam model which itself provides the only key to understanding how the whirlwind fifty-five days' victory was possible in March/April 1975.

CHAPTER 10

GIAP, THE GIANT-KILLER

Among the outstanding qualities of Ho Chi Minh was his capacity to attract men of similar stamp. Among the greatest of these was Vo Nguyen Giap. He was the only member of the top leadership I did not meet during my memorable first visit to Ho Chi Minh's headquarters in March 1954. 'Giap's rather busy elsewhere at the moment,' 'Uncle Ho' had said, rather apologetically. In fact, he was directing the opening phase of the battle of Dien Bien Phu, where he remained during the fifty-five days and nights of that historic battle. My first meeting with Giap took place in rather unusual circumstances.

Among the élite troops of the French Expeditionary Corps locked up in the Dien Bien Phu valley were Moroccan units. And among the Vietminh encircling them in the surrounding mountains was a Moroccan named Marouf, who had volunteered for service in Vietnam in order to desert to the Vietminh! His job was to follow up the sort of 'persuasion' work started by Nguyen Trai over 500 years earlier. (Doing the same sort of work was a German who had deserted from the Foreign Legion, and a couple of Frenchmen who had changed sides.) The Moroccans and other Muslim troops needed mutton from time to time to keep up their morale, so live lambs were occasionally dropped in with the parachuted supplies. As the Vietminh troops burrowed ever closer to the Dien Bien Phu headquarters of Colonel de Castries – promoted to the rank of brigadier-general during the battle to keep up *his* morale – Marouf wormed his way ever closer to the Moroccan troops. Over his megaphone Dien Bien Phu became an ironical 'Tiennent Bien Fous!' (Hang On You Dopes!), followed by instructions on how to desert, as quite a number of Moroccans and Algerians did. As the French perimeter shrunk, an ever greater proportion of supplies dropped into the Vietminh area. Among them was a lamb which fell almost at the feet of Marouf. It was decided that it should remain his. He kept it throughout the rest of the battle, later escorting it back to a special camp near Hanoi for Moroccans, Algerians and others who had responded to Marouf's 'persuasion' efforts. (Within less than a year, as a tribute to 'Uncle Ho's' internationalism and the military and political expertise of Marouf, most of the Algerians were taking part in armed struggle to liberate their own country from the French.) The lamb continued to wax fat on the choicest of green-stuffs at the farm school run by Marouf, reserved for a special occasion.

The special occasion was Tet (Lunar New Year's Day), 1955. As an Australian it was taken for granted that roasting a lamb was something I had been used to from childhood. Ashamed to admit the contrary, I accepted the task. A pit was dug for charcoal, a frame erected, a stout length of bamboo thrust through the length of the sacrificial creature and my vigil of giving it a quarter turn every fifteen minutes was marked, like a sand-glass for eggs, by a small glass of wine from Dien Bien Phu stocks.

Among the distinguished guests when the time came for scraping off the burned bits and getting at the meat was none other than the 'Tiger of Dien Bien Phu', Vo Nguyen Giap. Another was Pham Ngoc Thach, the French-trained medical scientist, then Deputy Minister, later Minister of Public Health. It was their first New Year in Hanoi for nine years and, for most of the rest of us, the first ever.

If it was the eyes of Ho Chi Minh, it was the forehead of Vo Nguyen Giap that commanded immediate attention.

Smooth, slightly bulging, it was a brow that expressed, above all, serenity. I made an immediate mental note: 'Unflappable'. A precious quality in a military man! Meat in those early post-Dien Bien Phu days in Hanoi was not very plentiful and both Giap and Pham Ngoc Thach remarked that it was not 'every day' that they ate it at all, let alone in such quantities as the fatted lamb provided. The occasion marked the beginning of a long and precious friendship with a person who, by all standards, must be considered one of the greatest military practitioners of all times.

In a typical burst of enthusiasm, after the devastating defeat of the US–Saigon invasion of southern Laos, in February 1971, Prince Norodom Sihanouk told me: 'Vo Nguyen Giap is a military genius, undoubtedly the greatest strategist of our time and one of the greatest of all time. He's a second Napoleon . . .' He reflected a moment and added: 'Greater than Napoleon because Napoleon lost battles. Giap always wins them.' It was not quite correct, but what is correct is that Giap did not lose wars, even such an impossibly unequal one as that with the United States. From 22 December 1944, when he led a ragged band of thirty-four men, significantly enough named the Tran Hung Dao platoon, to attack two posts in the northern border areas, to The 1975 Spring Offensive is a span of over thirty years which included ever-expanding victories against the foremost military powers of the day. An impressive performance, by any standards.

Like the father of Ho Chi Minh, the father of Giap was a peasant scholar-patriot. In 1924, at the age of twelve, young Giap was sent by his father from his native village of An Xa, in Quang Binh province, just north of the seventeenth parallel, to Hue, to study at the same Quoc Hoc college where Ho Chi Minh had studied some fifteen years earlier. He became involved in nationalist student activities and was expelled with the black mark of 'subversive' on his school record. His school years were marked by some of the first stirrings of a Vietnamese working class which was gradually forming. One of the first signs of this was a strike in the Saigon naval repair yards, which held up two French warships setting out for China in early 1925 to put down the Kuomintang-Communist forces preparing their march north against the Peking war-lord régime – and the international concession in Shanghai. The Saigon strike was frankly political, held in support of the Chinese revolution, and one of its leaders was Ton Duc Thang, hero of the Black Sea mutiny. There was also the agitation to force the French to cancel the death sentence passed on Phan Boi Chau and the demands to attend the funeral of Phan Chu Trinh. All of this captured the imagination of young Giap, as did the pamphlets circulating among the students signed by Nguyen Ai Quoc.

Giap flirted with various parties and organizations, seeking to identify himself with that which gave best promise of concrete action. His revolutionary path started to converge with that of Pham Van Dong who had been busy since returning from Canton, mobilizing students into the Revolutionary Youth League (Thanh Nien) training cadres and organizing underground trade unions. Two years of these activities produced a wave of strikes in 1929, in which workers in mines, plantations and factories all over the country, took part. But, as a result, Pham Van Dong was arrested and sentenced to ten years' imprisonment in Poulo Condor. For the average Vietnamese, considering the food and health conditions, the punishment was the equivalent of a death sentence. In fact, his dossier was endorsed to the effect that he should never be returned to the mainland!

Vo Nguyen Giap had attached himself to an Annam-based organization, the Tan Viet (an abbreviation for the Revolutionary Association of Annam). In February 1930, there was a bloody, but unsuccessful, uprising, at Yen Bai, in the north-western corner of the Red river delta. It was organized by the Quoc Dan Dang (National Revolutionary) Party, an approximate equivalent of the Chinese Kuomintang in its most progressive period. The uprising was repressed with great ferocity, virtually all the Quoc Dan Dang leaders being arrested and executed. It marked the end of another phase of the anti-French resistance struggle.

One week before the Yen Bai revolt, Nguyen Ai Quoc had presided over a meeting in Kowloon (the twin city of Hong Kong) between two factions of the Thanh Nien and one from the Tan Viet, each of which had transformed themselves into separate Communist parties. Nguyen Ai Quoc successfully persuaded them to reorganize into a single Vietnamese Communist Party. A few months later, at a conference in the Portuguese colony of Macao, this was enlarged into the Communist Party of Indochina. Vo Nguyen Giap was of the pro-Communist faction of the Tan Viet. In May of the same year, as a reaction to strong measures by the French to nip the newly formed Communist Party in the bud – especially in the urban areas – a Communist-led revolt took place resulting in the setting up of what became known as the Nghe An Soviet. It was crushed within a few months and among the results was the arrest and jailing of Giap for three years and the arrest of Ho Chi Minh in Hong Kong. He was saved from being handed over to the French – and certain execution – by the legal and extra-legal activities of a very courageous and upright British lawyer, Frank Loseby.

Giap, released from prison, apparently chastened and studious, started a law course at Hanoi University. With the election of a Popular Front government in France in 1936, a number of Vietnamese revolutionaries – including Pham Van Dong and Truong Chinh, who was later to become a member of the Political Bureau of the Vietnam Communist Party – were freed. However, the future president, Ton Duc Thang, was not released from Poulo Condor until the Vietminh seized power in August 1945, having served seventeen of a twenty years' sentence. After Pham Van Dong's release, he and Giap formed a political and personal friendship which has endured ever since. Later, during the crucial period when Ho Chi Minh was tramping from one Kuomintang jail to another or chained in filthy prison cells, it was these two who assumed the leadership and continuity of the Vietnamese revolution. In the meantime, under cover of his law studies at Hanoi University, Giap was secretly working with Truong Chinh on a fundamental work destined to set the original style of Vietnam's revolution.

A pamphlet, *The Revolutionary Road* (1925) that Nguyen Ai Quoc had written in Canton, using one of his other pseudonyms, had deeply impressed Giap, especially the phrase that:

'Revolution is the work of the broad masses of workers and peasants and not of a few individuals. Hence the necessity of organizing the masses.' Giap had grown up in the period when hopes were centred around names of individual scholar-patriots such as Phan Boi Chau, Phan Chu Trinh and others. And the hopes of countless of his generation were dashed when such leaders disappeared through death or arrest. But here was a new concept promising strength and continuity.

It was this that inspired Giap to start research with Truong Chinh into the role of the peasantry in Vietnamese history and contemporary society. The result was a two-volume work, *Van De Can Cay* (The Peasant Problem), signed by Van Dinh (Giap) and Qua Ninh (Truong Chinh), published, a volume at a time, in 1937–8, when the Popular Front government in France made such a venture possible.

It was the first thorough study of the economic, political, social and historical role of the peasantry, bringing into relief their revolutionary potential. Exposing the feudal repression to which the peasants were subject under colonialism and feudalism, the authors stressed the vital role the peasantry would play in the impending struggle for national independence. Shortly after the second – and more explosive – volume appeared, the Popular Front government collapsed and the local French administration ordered both volumes seized and destroyed. (The manuscript of a third volume, written by Truong Chinh alone, was seized by the French during one of their periodic man-hunts.) But the copies of the first two volumes which survived served as the basis for Communist Party, later Vietminh, policies towards the peasantry. Notably, reductions of land rent and taxes as the first steps towards land reform, and other policies which helped win over the peasantry as the main force for the long armed struggle that was being prepared. *The Peasant Problem* was a scholarly, analytical work in which one finds Giap's unlimited faith in the people, which in that period of Vietnam's development meant the peasantry, as the source of all strength, infinitely more powerful than weapons in the conventional sense of the term, not that Giap ever overlooked *their* importance.

Giap was unable to finish his law studies, partly due to lack of funds, partly due to his ever-increasing political activities. Early in 1938 he became a teacher of history at a private school in Hanoi, working on the side as a journalist for French- and Vietnamese-languge progressive papers. However, with the collapse of the Popular Front government and the banning of the Communist Party in France on the eve of World War II, the repression of Vietnamese progressives was greatly stepped up. And even more so once the war broke out. Some of the more exposed revolutionary activists had to leave the country, and so it was in May 1940, that Giap, together with Pham Van Dong, left for China. (Giap's first wife, Thai, was to join them but she was arrested and executed by the French.) When the two finally arrived in Kunming, they were advised by their comrades to await the arrival of Vuong, who was to decide what work they should do in China.

In the typical disciplined way of a Vietnamese revolutionary, Giap did not even enquire as to the real identity of Vuong, but he had a vague idea that it might be the legendary Nguyen Ai Quoc. He had been greatly impressed by the various texts signed by that name and also by P. C. Lin (another of Ho's pen-names). A month after their arrival in Kunming, Giap was invited to an outing at a lake on the city outskirts.

We were walking slowly along the shore when a middle-aged man, in a European suit and grey felt hat, approached. Phung Chi Kien introduced him: 'Comrade Vuong'. My intuitions were confirmed. It was none other than Nguyen Ai Quoc... I don't remember noticing anything striking or special about him as I had imagined I would. On the contrary, I found myself in the presence of a man of shining simplicity and this impression was only confirmed as time went by. I was meeting him for the first time, but immediately we felt linked by a deep friendship as if we had known each other for ages. I think that great men are always simple, simple in the sense that at first sight nothing particular stands out. One detail which I have never forgotten struck me. He spoke with a Central

115

Vietnam accent. I would never have thought that anyone who had been abroad so long would still retain his local accent.[1]

At subsequent meetings Nguyen Ai Quoc briefed Giap and others on the world situation, on what was going on in China and the development of the Sino–Japanese war. As to specifics, he advised Giap to go to Yenan and study politics at the training centre that he had set up there. He advised him also not to overlook military training. As things turned out Giap and Pham Van Dong never did reach Mao Tse-tung's headquarters at Yenan. While they were waiting for the Yenan-bound bus, France capitulated to the Germans and the Japanese were preparing to take over from the French in Indochina. Ho Chi Minh sent word to the two travellers to proceed to Kweilin, then the capital of Kwangsi province, which had a common frontier with the strategically important jungle-covered mountains north of the Red river delta, to be ready for important new developments which were bound to occur in Vietnam. There they had further meetings with Ho Chi Minh who explained that although for diplomatic reasons there must be relations with the Kuomintang, which was theoretically a potential ally because its armed forces were fighting the Japanese, utmost vigilance must be observed because of its fundamentally reactionary character. The warning was well merited because Chiang Kai-shek's troops, at about that time, launched an attack against the New Fourth Army, which, together with the Eighth Route Army, constituted the entirety of Mao Tse-tung's regular armed forces. Part of that attack took place against a New Fourth Army unit inside Kweilin itself. Giap and Pham Van Dong moved to Tsingsi, only 50 kms from the Vietnamese border, maintaining official contacts with the Kuomintang, while awaiting developments inside Vietnam. While in Kweilin there had been meetings with Nguyen Ai Quoc about a new, broader form of organization or national front, which they decided to call the Vietnam Independence League. But in its shortened form it became known as Vietminh. The proposal was duly

1. *Souvenirs sur Ho Chi Minh*, op cit, pp 176–83.

116

submitted to the Eighth Conference of the Party's Central Committee (held at Pac Bo in Vietnam's northern Cao Bang province in May 1941), and it was unanimously decided to promote the Vietminh as the overall resistance organization. On 19 September 1940, the Vichy government signed an agreement with Japan granting base and transit facilities in Vietnam, officially for pursuing its aggression against China. Ho Chi Minh, however, evaluated this as a Japanese move to swallow up Vietnam and the rest of Indochina as part of its expansionist aims. The Kuomintang was interested in using the Vietnamese revolutionaries as a counter to the Japanese penetration, but were not interested in supporting Communists in Vietnam or anywhere else. The Kuomintang had its own organization at Tsingsi to recruit Vietnamese – preferably from the largely defunct Quoc Dan Dang party – as agents for use against the Japanese in Vietnam. Giap and Pham Van Dong met a group of forty of these recruits as they were making their way from Cao Bang province to the Kuomintang training centre. In a typical 'persuasion' action, after long discussions, they convinced all of them that it was in the best interests of the nation to work with a genuine and national revolutionary organization such as theirs. After having received detailed instructions they returned to Vietnam and set up organizations of peasants, village elders, women and youths which were to become the first nuclei for mass organization throughout the country and the first base for armed resistance.

It was to take part in the Pac Bo Conference that Nguyen Ai Quoc had returned to Vietnam after thirty years of absence. Later in that fateful year of 1941, when the Japanese launched an all-out invasion of Indochina, the Vietminh leadership offered to join hands with the French, who still had plenty of armed forces in Vietnam, Laos and Cambodia, in resisting the Japanese. Instead the French joined hands with the Japanese in trying to exterminate the Vietminh. The latter started fighting the Japanese on their own, but allies were needed, which is why Nguyen Ai Quoc – adopting the name Ho Chi Minh for the first time – set off on a hazardous mission to Chungking to try to come to an arrangement with

Chiang Kai-shek. By this time he had French, Japanese and the Kuomintang police on his trail, which is why he adopted the new name.

From Tsingsi, where he was arrested by the Kuomintang police, he was escorted up and down the steep mountain roads to Nan-ning – now the Kwangsi provincial capital – and from there to Kweilin and on to Liuchow, in and out of thirty vermin-ridden prisons on the way. He jotted down four- and five-line poems to set the tone of each of his jails and his feelings as he stumbled up and down the roads from prison to prison. His revolutionary optimism could not be repressed even in the most impossible moments, as a sampling of some of the following poems reveals:

On the Road

Although they have tightly bound my arms and legs,
All over the mountains I hear the song of birds,
The forest filled with the perfume of spring flowers.
Who can prevent me from enjoying these,
Taking a little of the loneliness from the long journey?

Tungchun

Tungchun jail is much the same as Ping Ma:
Each meal a bowl of rice-gruel, the stomach always empty,
But water and light is here in abundance,
Each day the cells twice opened to let in fresh air.

Goodbye to a Tooth

You are hard and proud, my friend,
Not soft and long like the tongue:
Together we have shared the bitter and the sweet,
But now you must go west, while I go east.[2]

It was through such harsh personal experiences, as well as that of the nation, that caused Ho Chi Minh to launch the phrase which became the national watchword. 'Nothing is more Precious than Independence and Freedom', the simple

2. Ho Chi Minh, *Carnet de Prison* (Hanoi, 1971).

118

phrase later to be inscribed in letters of gold at the entrance to his Mausoleum!

While Ho was away, Giap and Pham Van Dong were doing their best to prepare for expanding armed struggle, first organizing village self-defence groups in Cao Bang and the other northern provinces. These were so effective that large regions gradually began to be linked up, into which neither French nor Japanese could penetrate. At the height of their preparatory work, a messenger arrived from Kwangsi – Ho Chi Minh had died in prison! Giap fainted at the messenger's feet. Fortunately there was soon a convincing denial that 'Uncle Ho' was still on his feet. By late 1942, Giap had formed a 'Vanguard Unit to Advance Southward', which was aimed at expanding outwards and southwards from the solidly consolidated base in Cao Bang. But once the components of this unit went beyond their home villages, and also their purely self-defensive functions, they began to run into trouble and take unacceptable losses. In other words Giap's military career was getting off to a bad start. In 1968, when Vo Nguyen Giap knew I was working on a book analysing some of the experiences of the Vietnamese revolution (*Vietnam Will Win*, Guardian Press, New York, 1969), he handed me a manuscript entitled *Liberation Army*, published in a very limited edition in Vietnamese in 1947, never translated because publishers considered it had been outdated by some of his subsequent works. However, apart from the picture of the problems of the day, it gives profound insight into Giap's thinking and his insistence on political over military aspects of warfare, as well as the difficulties of getting armed struggle off the ground in the 1940s. He explained that when the slogan of 'Armed Insurrection' was launched with the formation of the Vietminh in May 1941, there were many who doubted the feasibility of taking on the French and Japanese. But it was he and Pham Van Dong who went ahead and selected 'resolute elements' to be organized into self-defence groups.

These groups were formed from young volunteers and, according to the rules, everyone had to acquire a weapon of some sort, a bamboo spear, a club, a musket or flintlock and, if possible, find ways and means of getting hold of a rifle.

119

Giap, however, recognized that one of the greatest weaknesses in the revolutionary movement was the lack of military instructors, and, indeed, the problem of arming the groups was no less difficult. There were, in fact, plenty of muskets in the highlands and in the Red river delta but, from Giap's point of view, they were not always in the hands of politically-conscious people. In addition, the question of implanting confidence in primitive weapons against an enemy's modern arms was not an easy thing. But, even under these difficult conditions, preparations for a generalized armed uprising reached a very advanced state, and at a conference of Vietminh cadres from the three northern provinces of Cao Bang, Bac Can and Lang Son, in June 1944, the date was set for launching co-ordinated armed struggle.

Just as the first shots were about to be fired, Giap very nearly fainted a second time. An ill and emaciated Ho Chi Minh staggered in from the jungle shadows and immediately cancelled the whole thing. He had finally been released from Liuchow, after two years of detention, to find his way back to the Cao Bang base. After listening to Giap's enthusiastic report and the detailed preparations for armed action, 'Uncle Ho' said it must be immediately called off and his authority was such that there was no question of going against his judgement. But Giap notes in *Liberation Army* that: 'On receipt of this new order and without understanding the reason, cadres were very unhappy, very irritated. Just as the dawn rays were beginning to shine through they were suddenly extinguished.' Ho considered that the political preparations were insufficient; that the military concepts were wrong; that the first action must absolutely be assured of success and of such a nature as to electrify the whole country; that all cadres should be psychologically prepared for the implications of a long struggle. Giap was given a lesson in the importance of not relying, as a main force, on dispersed guerilla groups, but to have one concentrated attack force capable of striking with superior strength at the selected target.

On a couple of sheets of paper, Ho laid down the guidelines which were to confound the military and political establishments of France and the United States for the thirty years that

120

followed. Emphasis on the political effect of all military action was the keynote of Ho's strategy and he insisted that the first strike unit of the future Vietnam People's Army should be named 'Propaganda Brigade of the Vietnamese Liberation Army', which, wrote Ho in his directive, 'means that the political activity of the brigade is more important than its military efforts'. The directive laid down three points:

1. Above all it carries out propaganda. In military affairs, in order to function efficiently, the fundamental principle is to regroup existing forces. Thus, according to new directives of our organization, it will be necessary to choose the most ardent elements from the Bac Can, Lang Son and Cao Bang guerilla groups and set up our main brigade. We will give the latter the greater part of available arms.

   Our resistance being of a popular character, we can mobilize and arm the whole people. That is why at the same time that we regroup our forces to set up the first brigade, we should think about retaining the regional forces, co-ordinating their activities and helping them in all possible ways. The brigade must back up the regional cadres, look after their training, provide them with weapons when possible and do everything to enable the regional forces to expand.

2. Regarding the regional forces, regroup cadres to train them, afterwards send them to the various local regions, carry out exchange of experiences, maintain close liaison between units, co-ordinate their combat activities.

3. Concerning tactics, practise guerilla methods: secrecy, speed, initiative – today in the East, tomorrow in the West – appear and disappear by surprise, without leaving a trace. The Propaganda Brigade of the Vietnamese Liberation Army is, called upon to become the eldest of a large family. May it see new brigades born as quickly as possible to support it!

   Modest, to be sure, at the beginning, but opening up before it are the most glorious perspectives. It is the embryo of the Liberation Army, with the whole territory from North to South as its field of activities.[3]

'Initiative, speed, secrecy,' remarks Giap in his *Liberation Army*, 'simple words to express the essence of a guerilla's stock-in-trade. President Ho paid great attention to secrecy. It was imperative to preserve absolute secrecy, to conceal our forces well, disorient the enemy. It is essential that the enemy underestimate our strength, that he completely ignore our activities. At the beginning, when we decided to collect certain equipment from the imperialist troops to camouflage and disguise our own, the President advised us to show ourselves, even in disguise, only in case of absolute necessity; better not to show ourselves at all. That could only attract the enemy's attention and secrecy could be lost. When we received our first mission, the President wrote us twice again recommending "you must maintain secrecy . . ."'

It was Giap who was charged with heading the first brigade (in fact a platoon of thirty-four men) in the historic first military action. On the night of 22 December 1944, his primitively armed band – divided into two groups – simultaneously attacked the two French forts of Phay Kat and Na Ngan in Cao Bang province, wiping out the garrisons and seizing all arms and equipment. The date has since been celebrated as the birthday of what was to become the Vietnam People's Army.

'Having received our orders,' Giap wrote in *Liberation Army*, 'we were able to mobilize 34 cadres and members of regional armed groups with two muskets, 17 rifles, 14 flintlocks and Chinese arms. It was fortunate for us that two days previously we had received from a Monsieur Tong Minh Phuong, a Vietnamese living in Kunming, an American machine-gun with 150 cartridges, 6 fuse bombs, a case of time-bombs and 500 piastres for expenses . . .'

Thus was launched the armed struggle which was only to end on 30 April 1975. Four months after the attack on the two French posts, the various armed groups which immediately sprang into activity were fused into the Liberation Army,

3. Translated from Ho Chi Minh, *Oeuvres Choisies du Président Ho Chi Minh* (Hanoi. 1962), pp 28–9.

122

later the Vietnam People's Army which has functioned until this day under the Central Military Committee founded in April 1946. Its Chairman was – and still is – Vo Nguyen Giap and two of its leading members were the former Hanoi textile worker, Van Tien Dung and a guerilla leader of the Nung ethnic minority, Chu Van Tan.

Within eight months the armed forces had developed to a point at which, taking advantage of the collapse of the Axis powers and the impending surrender of the Japanese, the Vietminh seized power throughout Vietnam within a few days, starting from 15 August 1945. They disarmed all Japanese troops, locking them up for handing over to the Allied forces. The French returned in force towards the end of 1945 and after endless negotiations and promises of independence, during which time the French continued to build up their forces, they tried to crush Vietminh forces in the South in late 1945 and in the North a few months later. After eight to nine years of full-scale war, the French admitted defeat by signing the Geneva Agreement on 20 July 1954. Once they had extricated their Expeditionary Corps in the North from a situation made untenable by the Dien Bien Phu defeat, they turned their backs on the political clauses of the Geneva Agreement, the essential clause of which provided for elections by 20 July 1956, to reunify the country. The United States, which took part in the Geneva negotiations, but refused to sign the Agreement, had set up a client régime, under Ngo Dinh Diem, in Saigon, during the Geneva negotiations, and started to take over from the French as the dominant power in South Vietnam. It encouraged the Diem régime to refuse to implement the Agreement, publicly applauding when, in 1955, Diem declared his government was no longer bound by it. Large-scale repression of former Vietminh members and their suspected sympathizers in the South led to armed resistance, sporadic and spontaneous at first, but generalized and organized after the setting up of the National Liberation Front of South Vietnam in December 1960.

The rapid military-political successes of the NLF resulted in US military intervention at the end of 1961, in the form of military 'advisers'. By 1964, these totalled 22,000 and were directing military operations, together with US air support, down to battalion and company level.

Following the continuing defeats of the US–Saigon forces, which assumed disastrous proportions in early 1965, the United States started its air war against North Vietnam in February 1965, and the commitment of its own combat forces in South Vietnam the following month. These were gradually built up to a peak of 550,000 men. Following what became known as the Tet (Lunar New Year) Offensive by the NLF – by then supported by North Vietnamese troops – early in 1968, which was a very severe setback for the US–Saigon forces, the US Field Commander, General Westmoreland, was removed, President Johnson refused to commit any more US troops, accepted a North Vietnamese offer of negotiations and announced that he would not contest the 1968 presidential elections. After much diplomatic skirmishing, negotiations started in Paris in May 1968, between the United States and North Vietnam. These ended in agreement on the eve of the US presidential elections with the USA committed to end the bombings of North Vietnam and by both sides agreeing to open full-scale negotiations with the participation of the Saigon government and the NLF which, in the meantime, had established a Provisional Revolutionary Government (PRG). Following almost five years of protracted negotiations an agreement was eventually signed in Paris on 27 January 1973 to end the war in Vietnam. It was subsequently signed by the foreign ministers of the four negotiating powers, by Britain and the Soviet Union as co-chairmen of the 1954 Geneva Conference, by France and People's China as signatories of the 1954 Geneva Conference, and by Canada, Poland, Hungary and Indonesia, the latter four in their capacity as members of an International Commission which was to supervise the implementation of the Agreement. President Nguyen Van Thieu of South Vietnam, who had won out in a power struggle with many of his rivals to become Head of State, announced his refusal to implement the Agreement and launched innumerable operations to wipe out the NLF forces. As US troops and air power were gradually withdrawn, Thieu's efforts, after some preliminary success, were obviously even less effective than before. Once the United States had retrieved several hundreds of its pilots shot down over North Vietnam, it showed no interest in pressurizing President Thieu to implement the Paris Agreement. Thieu continued to act as if he believed a battlefield solution was possible.

CHAPTER 11

BEGINNING THE END

It was as a result of the failure of the 1973 Paris Agreement that at 10.30 am on 5 February 1975, a Soviet Antonov 24 took off from Hanoi's Gia Lam airport. The curious might have wondered why the head of North Vietnam's air force, Brigadier-General Le Van Try and the Deputy Chief of Staff of the Armed Forces, Brigadier-General Phung The Tai, were on hand for an emotional farewell to the chief passenger, whose code name was *Tuan*. It headed directly south and passenger *Tuan* was to continue heading south long after he left the plane at the totally destroyed fishing port of Dong Hoi. His departure was kept even more secret than that of Vo Nguyen Giap and Pham Van Dong thirty-five years earlier. And it continued to be kept secret, because, at Dong Hoi, he changed from the uniform of a senior officer of the Vietnam People's Army into the *baba* or 'black pyjama' so closely associated with the Vietcong. But Giap and Dong were hiding their departure from their enemies and heading north; *Tuan* was hiding his from his own comrades and heading south. His real name was General Van Tien Dung, Chief of Staff of the Vietnam People's Army.

Every day for a couple of weeks following his departure, his black Soviet Volga, with the back seat curtains drawn as usual, travelled from his residence to the General Staff Headquarters, making the return journey, also as usual, sometime between midday and 5 pm. In the evenings soldiers from the Headquarters staff came to play volleyball with their commander – but were disciplined enough not to ask why he was absent! Messages to congratulate the Soviet Union and the German Democratic Republic on the anniversary of the founding of their armed forces were sent out in General Van Tien Dung's name as usual, also to the Mongolian People's Republic the following month.

The departure was just five days before Tet, the Lunar New Year, but old comrades received their cards and presents with the familiar signature on the eve of the great national fête. 'Uncle Ho's' injunctions on enforcing absolute secrecy in all phases of military activity had never been forgotten. The Vietnamese leadership never underestimated their enemy, especially his capacity for information assessment. There were numerous embassies in Hanoi whose specialized personnel kept tabs on the movements of the country's leaders, especially the military ones. So there were routine items in the press indicating the continuing presence there of the Chief of Staff.

Not likely to forget Ho Chi Minh's twice-repeated warning before his own first military engagement, Vo Nguyen Giap could be relied upon to go to extreme lengths in this respect when he sent his chief aide south to direct the supreme climactic event in Vietnam's 2000 years of military campaigning. Among other aspects, the thirty-year-long comradeship-in-arms between Giap, whose code name in the impending operation was *Chien*, and *Tuan* was now to be put to its severest test. Giap would direct from the rear headquarters, Dung would command from the spot. Thus Van Tien Dung and his staff – the whole group under the code name of A-75 – left Hanoi, their destination and task known only to those required to know. Those included, above all, the Political Bureau of what was then the Lao Dong or Workers' Party – in fact, the Communist Party – of which the general-secretary was Le Duan, and its Central Military Committee, still headed by Vo Nguyen Giap.

The elaborate measures to conceal Dung's absence from

128

Hanoi were not the only ones calculated to throw dust in the watchful eyes of Saigon and Washington. 'The Americans love captured documents', Premier Pham Van Dong was to tell me after it was all over, adding: 'Well we made sure they got plenty.' Thus it was that, at a two-day conference held by President Nguyen Van Thieu with his top army and regional commanders in Saigon on 9–10 December 1974, to assess the adversary's intentions and capacities for the forthcoming year, the conclusion was that they could only be limited in scope. They could not reach the dimensions of the Tet Offensive of 1968 (when all four zonal headquarters of the US–Saigon military command were simultaneously attacked, together with eight out of the eleven divisional headquarters, thirty-seven of what were then forty provincial capitals, two American field headquarters and – among eighteen major targets in Saigon – the US embassy partially occupied by guerilla commandos). They could not repeat the 1972 Spring Offensive, when the US–Saigon's 'Maginot Line' south of the North–South demarcation line along the seventeenth parallel was overrun and the provincial capital of Quang Tri was temporarily captured. In 1975, no provincial capitals would be lost, and even if some were it would only be for a very short spell.

The military commanders in Saigon concluded that Hanoi would try to extend the area under PRG (Provisional Revolutionary Government of South Vietnam) control in the Central Highlands and in the Mekong delta, to put pressure on Saigon to implement the terms of the Agreement signed in Paris on 27 January 1973 to end the war. There would be an attempt, according to this assessment, by the adversary to seize Tay Ninh, capital of the province of that name, about 70 kms north-west of Saigon and to transform it into the PRG's own capital. The operations would start about the Lunar New Year and would continue at most until the start of the rainy season in May/June. Therefore, the overall decision made was that the Saigon forces should strike first and knock the enemy off balance. It was agreed that a three months' 'immediate accelerated pacification' campaign should be launched as from New Year's Day 1975. As usual, the whole of the proceedings of the conference were known in Hanoi. (The extent of the penetration into the Saigon Command's military apparatus at all levels was such that the maximum delay of knowledge of their decisions from High Command to tactical operational level was four hours.) It was another of those comforting illustrations of the superiority of man over the machines he creates. Thieu and his generals had the benefit of the most super-sophisticated gadgetry of detection and computerized projections of enemy planning that American technical genius could devise. The Pentagon placed it all at Thieu's disposal. Giap had a network of skilled, courageous men at the place he needed to report back on *his* enemy's intentions. Thieu *thought* he knew what were Giap's plans; Giap *knew* he knew of Thieu's! A battle-winning and war-winning difference!

As usual Giap struck with devastating rapidity once the enemy's assessment of his plans was evaluated. Four days after the end of the Saigon strategy meeting, the district town of Duc Phong, in Phuoc Long province, about 140 kms due north of Saigon, and the same distance north-east of Tay Ninh, was attacked and captured. Not surprisingly, Saigon was caught totally unawares. On 22 December, the same fate for the district centre of Bo Duc and four days later that of Don Luan. The whole of Phuoc Long province, except the provincial capital of Phuoc Binh, had been lost in just twelve days. Reinforcements were rushed to hold the capital but it also fell on 6 January 1975. Thus, a whole province, including its capital, was lost for the first time in a war which had been going on intermittently, but with ever-increasing violence, since 1954. In Hanoi, Giap and Dung folded their arms and studied the reactions. Their evaluations of these were to be crucial for the months to come; decisive in fixing the date for the departure of *Tuan* for the South.

Why the crisis and why the timing? After nearly five years of negotiations, an Agreement to end the war in Vietnam had been signed in Paris. Essentially it had been worked out in a mammoth series of secret, followed by not-so-secret, talks between US Secretary of State, Henry Kissinger, and senior member of North Vietnam's Political Bureau (of the Lao

Dong Party), Le Duc Tho. Objectively that Agreement was an historic triumph for Le Duc Tho, especially in view of last-minute maximum pressure by the Nixon–Kissinger 'Christmas bombings' of Hanoi by B52 bombers which preceded by just one month the signing of the Agreement. The bombings were intended to force Hanoi to downgrade the first sentence of the Draft Agreement, 'The United States and all other countries respect the independence, sovereignty, unity and territorial integrity of Vietnam as recognized by the 1954 Geneva Agreements on Vietnam', to a place much further down in the Agreement. It was to retain it in first place that the North Vietnamese leadership took on the B52s. However, the Agreement was never acceptable to Saigon's Nguyen Van Thieu as he repeatedly stated, loudly and publicly. It was alleged – and not refuted – in South Vietnam's National Assembly, that Thieu had accepted a seven-million-dollar bribe to mollify his objections and to bring him to sign on the dotted line.

Apart from providing for the withdrawal of remaining American troops – which was done – and military advisers, technicians – which was not done – the Agreement laid down procedures for a political settlement in South Vietnam based on general elections supervised by a 'National Council of National Reconciliation and Concord' representing a Third Force, not tied to either the PRG (Vietcong) or the Saigon régime, which would play the key mediating role. There would be a demarcation of the military zones under the control of the PRG and Saigon forces respectively, release of military and political prisoners detained by each side – ar d of American POW pilots held in North Vietnam and others held in the South. Like the 1954 Geneva Agreement, it was very good on paper. But as in 1954, with the French, once the Americans got the POWs back and their combat forces safely extricated from impossible situations, the rest of the Agreement was ignored. The 'National Council' was never set up; Thieu declared there was no such thing as a 'Third Force' and did his best to prove it by wiping out or jailing all suspected to be 'neutralist'. He also launched a series of military operations into PRG-controlled areas, refusing to acknowledge any demarcation of military zones. He also dismissed any question of elections held under any supervisory body other than his own government or under any conditions other than those laid down by himself. It appears that the Nixon–Kissinger administration backed him to the hilt, despite the fact they had signed the Paris Agreement – as distinct from that of Geneva (in which they had promised 'not to use force or the threat of force' to upset).

At a meeting I had with Premier Pham Van Dong a couple of weeks after the signing of the Paris Agreement, and after he had studied Saigon and Washington reactions to the signing, he commented grimly: 'Our experience after signing so many unfulfilled agreements is that if the other side does not fulfil them we have to fulfil them ourselves.' A very portentous remark as it turned out!

On the eve of the year of the Tiger (1974) – the lunar new year traditionally being a time for assessing events in the old year and trying to foresee those in the year ahead – there was a very special meeting at the Hanoi headquarters of the VPA, at 33 Pham Ngu Lao Street.[1] Before the cream of the officers' corps – army and divisional commanders, heads of the political and intelligence departments of the High Command and of all branches of the armed forces – Le Duan and Le Duc Tho gave a briefing on the real essence of a resolution adopted in October 1973 by the Lao Dong Party's Central Committee. President Ton Duc Thang made an unusual appearance, for that type of meeting, and together with the reports of the Party Secretary-General, Le Duan, and the senior member of the Politbureau, Le Duc Tho, this was taken, in the words of Van Tien Dung, 'as the equivalent of an order from the Party and the State to the armed forces: "Advance! . . ." '

Their armed forces in the South, following the signature of the Paris Agreement, had received strict orders to observe a

1. Pham Ngu Lao was the warrior son-in-law of the immortal Tran Hung Dao who thrice thrashed the Mongols. Anyone who thinks that Vietnam's history started with the Bolshevik or Chinese Communist revolutions only has to stroll around the boulevards and streets of Hanoi, the finest of them named after their own – and not others' – revolutionary heroes. Not only those of the battlefield but, as Ho Xuan Huong Street demonstrates, heroes and heroines of their literature and poetry. It is in this spirit also that one must understand the renaming of Saigon as Ho Chi Minh City.

132

bamboo-type behaviour, to 'bend but not break'. To fall back when Saigon forces attacked, at the risk of losing some valuable territory, in order to prove which side was for peace, which for continued war; which for upholding the Paris Agreement, which for sabotaging it. This was in accordance with 'Uncle Ho's' overall principle that every military action must be measured by its political effect. Even retreats and what could be construed as defeats could be counted as victories if the political effect was positive. The people wanted peace, was the overall assessment, and would eventually turn against those who insisted on continuing the war. Accordingly territory was lost and the Saigon régime to many seemed to have gained the upper hand. Instructions, however, were always to defend base areas to limit the damage. Following the October 1973 resolution, a 'thus far and no further' order-of-the-day was issued, instructing all units to hold their ground and resist any further encroachments. This was followed by another, a month later, to take back lost territory and 'punish' enemy bases from which attacks into PRG-controlled territory were launched.

The net result of the conference in Hanoi was that, as it was clear that the Paris Agreement would never be implemented, preparations must be made to 'fulfil it ourselves', as Pham Van Dong had expressed it.

How does one set about such a task? It was a question discussed many times between Giap and Dung and their staff officers before Dung's departure, and again in the Antonov 24, by the A-75 team, as they set out on their historic mission. Because of the assessment of Thieu and his officers in Saigon, the general disposition of their armed forces had not greatly been changed. Of the four military regions – the 1st starting south of the Seventeenth Parallel and the 4th furthest south in the Mekong delta – the heaviest concentration of the best troops was in the 1st and 3rd regions, the latter guarding the all-important approaches to Saigon. The 2nd military region which included mainly the Central Highlands and a small part of the Coastal Plains was relatively lightly defended. Of Saigon's thirteen regular divisions, five were in the 1st, three in the 3rd, another three in the 4th and only two in the

2nd military region, with a proportionate number of supporting troops in each, except that the 2nd region had a relatively greater number of planes and armoured vehicles. Altogether, the Saigon Command had at its disposal 1,351,000 men, including 495,000 regular and 475,000 regional troops, plus 381,000 civil guards (village militia). No figures are available for the forces at Van Tien Dung's disposal at the time he started to head south, but a generally accepted estimate was about 350,000, a number soon greatly increased by regular divisions of the VPA. It was significant that waiting on the Dong Hoi airstrip was General Dong Si Nguyen, commander of Unit 559 (which, in the coding that only VPA and support units understand, means that it was formed in May 1959.)

If one wanted to put a finger on the single most important war-winning weapon – apart from the errors of US military and political strategists – it would have to be Unit 559, which built, maintained and continually expanded what became known as the 'Ho Chi Minh Trail'. It was on this unit, above all others, that *Tuan* would have to depend to successfully carry out his assignment. To go back to the origin of Unit 559, one would have to go back to the days of the anti-French resistance war, when the far-seeing 'Uncle Ho' asked for volunteers among war orphans to go and make their lives among the ethnic minorities of the Central Highlands. They were warned that it would be tough. They must be prepared for total integration, accepting such local customs as filing the teeth down to gum level, eating putrid meat, observing the rigid taboos regarding women and, in general, practising the 'three withs' (living, working, eating) on local terms. Only thus could the confidence of the Montagnards be won – it would not be a temporary assignment, but a lifetime's vocation. Such was the confidence in 'Uncle Ho' that a sizeable number took up the challenge, went to the Central Highlands, adopted local customs and won the confidence of a high proportion of the tribal peoples. Had they not, Unit 559's task would have been impossible, and that of *Tuan* even more so.

In May 1959, while Central Committee members of the Lao Dong Party in Hanoi were still divided as to whether armed struggle should be supported in the South, Ho Chi Minh took the initiative in demanding that, at the very least, a transport and communications route be opened up. The re-opening of the existing north–south road and railway, cut at the Ben Hai river on the Seventeenth Parallel, was indefinitely postponed by the refusal of the Saigon régime to hold the reunification elections in July 1956, as specified in the 1954 Geneva Agreement. The future 'Ho Chi Minh Trail' would therefore 'bend' around the demarcation line into territory controlled by Ho Chi Minh's allies – the Pathet Lao in Laos – and would lead back into territory controlled by friendly ethnic minorities in South Vietnam. (By that time there were sporadic and spontaneous revolts against the Saigon régime by tribal groups friendly to the 'Vietminh' during the anti-French war, but armed struggle was still frowned upon by the majority of Lao Dong Central Committee members, until Le Duan arrived from the South and secured majority support for his contention that without armed struggle the entire revolutionary infrastructure would be wiped out to the last man and woman. Vietnam would remain partitioned for the foreseeable future.) Any north–south route through the only politically accessible areas would have to crawl in and around and through the formidable Annamite mountain chain, known to the Vietnamese as the Truong Son mountains which run almost the full length of Vietnam from the China border to the Mekong river delta, forming, for part of the way, Vietnam's frontier with Laos and Cambodia.

Once again an appeal was made for volunteers, exceptionally sound of health, mind and ideology, ready for very dangerous and arduous work, for malaria and other diseases and for long separation from home and family. As usual in Vietnam's history when danger from outside threatened, there was no lack of response. From the tens of thousands of volunteers, the Truong Son unit, also named 559, was formed in May 1959.

By the spring of 1975, after sixteen years of back-breaking work by the unit, many sections of the trail had been macadamized, indeed, in many places, the former mountain track had become a highway, with many of its sections 8 ms wide. The total length exceeded 20,000 kms, forming a thick network of strategic and operational roads, with 5000 kms of oil pipelines crossing rivers, streams and mountain passes, many of them over 1000 ms high. It was one of history's great military engineering feats, comparable to the building of the Burma Road by the Chinese, linking the Burmese railhead of Lashio with Kunming and the Kuomintang capital of Chungking, after the Japanese had denied China any external supplies by occupying all the coastal ports.

So it was that, escorted by a convoy of Unit 559 vehicles, Task Force A-75 moved south, crossing the Ben Hai river on the Seventeenth Parallel which still theoretically separated North and South Vietnam, then heading for Unit 559 headquarters about 25 kms south-west of the Ben Hai, towards the Laotian frontier. Van Tien Dung's first reflection on seeing the start of the network of motorable highways leading south was to lament that Tran Dang Ninh, a veteran Vietminh expert of moving supplies, 'the real creator of our Logistics Department had not lived to see the realization of his dreams'. For in his day logistics was expressed in the ton-kilometre capacity of ox carts, bicycles and human backs!

> At the beginning of 1975, our roads and tracks were dotted with over 10,000 trucks, some belonging to the Army, the others sent as reinforcements by the Ministry of Transport. Our logistics service, while satisfying our annual needs, had been able to economize and accumulate, day after day and month after month and on the whole of our fronts in the South, reserve stocks in anticipation of the Great Day. '559' had fulfilled its duties towards our own troops and our international obligations towards the fraternal countries (Laos and Cambodia). Nothing was more stimulating than to see our fighting men now being moved by motorized transport and getting a decent meal right up to the front line. Even our dry rations, such as the A72, were very palatable.[2]

How had a Hanoi textile worker become involved in such

2. Van Tien Dung, *Dai Than Mua Xuan* (The Great Spring Offensive) Hanoi, 1976), p 51. Translated from the Vietnamese.

an enterprise at all? Why did he think he could pull it off against American- and French-trained professionals, advised by the best strategists and tacticians that the Pentagon could put at Saigon's disposal? Vietnamese leaders are very reticent to talk about themselves and Van Tien Dung was no exception when I put the question as to whether there was any specific incident that had turned him into a revolutionary, or whether there was any special reason why he should have been chosen to command the most momentous of all military confrontations of the previous thirty years. To both questions he replied with soldierly bluntness in the negative: 'No special reason!' However, he went on to explain:

Even when I was very young, I clearly saw the need for independence and was inspired by tales about my elders who had sacrified themselves for this. But when I became a textile worker, cruelly exploited like all the other work- ers, I saw that the struggle for national independence had to be tied in with that for socialism. That our people had not only to be in control of our country, but also of its economy. It was this conviction that led me to become a revolutionary and to ask for arms to fight for what I believed in, and to ask for military training to use those arms effectively. In the period from 1936–9 there was a great upsurge of militant activity, including strikes in many enterprises. I took part in that movement and this year, 1977, marks the fortieth anniversary of my mem- bership of the Communist Party. As an ardent militant it was natural to ask for, and to receive, military training.

I then put the question which always intrigued me and to which only such grass-roots revolutionaries as Van Tien Dung could supply the answer. Entirely brought up under a French educational system and an administration which had little interest in helping the Vietnamese to discover their past, did people of Van Tien Dung's generation know about the strug- gles of their ancestors? Did they draw their inspiration from that, or from the Russian and Chinese revolutions? The precise question was: 'To what extent were you and your

137

generation, obviously including men under your command, aware of the heroic struggles of your ancestors against foreign invaders ? Neither the French in their time, nor the Americans in theirs, had any interest in facilitating access to such knowledge!' Van Tien Dung smiled and agreed that my latter assumption was correct. But:

Details of the heroic struggles of our ancestors throughout the centuries were handed down from mouth to mouth, in terms of legends and accounts from fathers to their children, of the deeds of *their* fathers, grandfathers, great-grandfathers and still further back. Our history of resistance was also known from books to those who had access to them. Some aspects were included in history text-books used in the schools – even in South Vietnam . . . But for my generation, and that of my father, one thing was always clear. Vietnamese soil must always belong to Vietnamese and our ancestors had always fought defensive wars for this principle.

As to why a former, almost illiterate textile worker was on his way to command the most momentous military campaign since Dien Bien Phu, but on an infinitely greater scale, my mind goes back to the ceremonial entry into Hanoi, on 12 October 1954, of the city's 'own' regiment. There was great excitement as relatives started to recognize sons and husbands who had left Hanoi almost eight years previously, in rags and tatters, carrying their wounded with them, after two months of barricade and house-to-house fighting against the powerfully armed French. The tattered heroes of the barricade battalion were the nucleus around which was built the Hanoi Regiment, later part of the élite 308th Division. Organizer of that battalion and later commander of the 308th, was Van Tien Dung. Shortly after he had taken the 'revolutionary road' as he expressed it, he had shown a natural aptitude for military affairs, great organizational ability and courage which is why 'Uncle Ho' made him a member of the Central Military Committee, and he soon became Vo Nguyen Giap's right-hand man.

138

CHAPTER 12

WHY BUON ME THUOT?

Why was Buon Me Thuot chosen as the opening target in the campaign that was to end the war? The choice was absolutely unexpected as far as the Saigon Command was concerned and received only lukewarm support at first from some of Giap's field commanders and even from within the High Command. Vietnamese revolutionaries, fortunately, are of a very independent mind, challenging propositions and even decisions made by their superiors with which they cannot intellectually or politically agree. Buon Me Thuot, a drowsy city of mainly Montagnard population, about 250 kms north-east of Saigon and 50 kms from the Cambodian border, certainly occupies a strategic position on the plateaux of the Central Highlands. So important, in fact, that the Americans considered making it a fall-back capital in case Saigon had to be abandoned. Properly developed militarily, from Buon Me Thuot the three countries of Indochina could be dominated by unlimited use of air power. So ran the American argument. In any case, it had been developed into a formidable military bastion.

In October 1974, there had been another of those momentous meetings of the Politbureau and the Central Military Committee in Hanoi, this time to enable Giap and Dung and

some of their top aides to give a briefing on the strategic
operational plans they had worked out on the basis of the
'green light' they had received at the earlier meeting on the
eve of the New Year of the Tiger. Van Tien Dung describes
some aspects of the meeting:

October 1974: The first end-of-autumn freshness re-
minded us that the opening of the campaign would not
be long delayed . . . With the aid of maps, diagrams,
charts of comparative statistics that covered the four
walls of the conference room; with detailed reports on
developments on the various battle-fronts up till October
1974, the operational service gave as exhaustive a briefing
as possible on the overall situation. After discussion, the
conference arrived at a unanimous, five-point summing-
up of the situation made by Le Duan:

1. The military, political and economic weakening of the
   puppet army was only increasing. In the South our
   forces had now acquired incontestable superiority
   over the enemy.

2. The United States, hampered by the increasing difficulties encountered at home and abroad, had to re-
   duce their capabilities of aid to the Saigon régime in
   the political as well as the economic field. It would be
   very difficult for them to return in force to South
   Vietnam and, even supposing they did so, they could
   never save the Saigon régime from total collapse.

3. By increasing our effectives and supplies and by
   reinforcing our network of strategic and operational
   roads, we had achieved a communications link-up
   which enabled us to exploit in our favour the dynamics
   of our superiority.

4. The movements in favour of peace, of improvement of
   living conditions, for democratic rights, for national
   independence and the departure of Thieu, were being
   stepped up in the cities.

140

5. The just cause for which our people were fighting enjoyed the sympathy and support from people all over the world.[1]

The 'just cause'! How often this had been evoked as a weapon since Ly Bi, in the middle of the seventh century, had baptized his army as the 'troops of the just cause'! It became an absolute constant as a rallying cry during thirteen centuries of armed struggle. At first to mobilize people at home, later to mobilize them abroad. Dung, in his book, goes on to relate that the meeting brushed aside the question of renewed US intervention – and this included the possibility of renewed air attacks against the North which it was known could be withstood. Then the conferees agreed on the General Staff's proposal that the initial area of operations should be Saigon's No. 2 Tactical Zone – the Central Highlands – but that the details, including the first target of attack, should be the object of further study. Another crucial conference took place between 18 December 1974 and 8 January 1975, this time together with key cadres from the South. They included Politbureau member, Pham Hung,[2] two army corps commanders, Generals Tran Van Tra and Chu Huy Man, and two veteran members of the Central Committee from the South, Vo Chi Cong and Phan Van Dang. It was while this conference was in session, that the offensive in Phuoc Long province – mentioned in the previous chapter – took place. For the first time, there was indecision, even dissensions, within the Saigon High Command. What to do with a whole province, capital and all, lost? Launch a major operation to recapture at least the provincial capital? Regroup and concentrate forces in expectation of worse to come – a drive on Saigon for example! These were

1. *Dai Thang Mua Xuan*, op cit, pp 26–7.

2. In 1931, Pham Hung, together with one of the two vice-presidents of today's Socialist Republic of Vietnam, Le Van Luong, had spent seven months in the 'death row' of Saigon's central prison, expecting to be called any day to mount the steps to the guillotine. Eventually their death sentences were commuted to life imprisonment on Poulo Condor – which normally meant a longer version of the same thing. But together with Pham Van Dong, Truong Chinh and others, they were released when the Popular Front government came to power in France in 1936.

the key options discussed. In the end indecision prevailed and nothing was done. United States reaction was limited to sending a 7th Fleet Task Force, centred round the nuclear-powered aircraft-carrier *Enterprise*, into Vietnamese waters and placing the Okinawa-based 3rd Marine Division in a state of 'red alert'.

Every move in Saigon and Washington was immediately relayed to Hanoi, studied and analysed with the keenest attention at the planning conference. It was clear that Saigon was on the verge of a top level 'nervous breakdown'. And Washington was only capable of psychological warfare noises. In summing up the situation immediately after the Phuoc Long victory, and in view of the dithering in Saigon and Washington, Le Duan presented a most optimistic appraisal, reflecting the unanimous view of all those taking part in the conference. The enemy was on the ropes. It was necessary to hit him harder and faster than even their most optimistic planning had provided for till then. But even in his most exuberant forecasts, Le Duan could not imagine the tempo at which things were to develop.

'The situation is clear,' he said in his summing-up report. 'We are determined to complete our plan within two years...'[3] Which would have placed victory in the spring of 1977. Van Tien Dung said that he added reflectively: 'Two years perhaps is too short, but perhaps also too long!' Van Tien Dung's written account of that historic meeting states that Le Duan pointed out the necessity of stepping up pressures by local forces on all fronts from just south of the Seventeenth Parallel to the Mekong delta. This was in order to keep the enemy bogged down in defensive operations in all four military regions, including the sensitive areas in and around Saigon. He then came to the crucial point:

> 'We are agreed that the initial attack should be in the Central Highlands – this year.' Pointing to the map behind him, he added: 'We must open the campaign with an absolutely certain knockout blow at Buon Me Thuot and Tuy Hoa and swiftly follow up this first success...

3. *Dai Thang Mua Xuan*, op cit, p 32.

'Whatever the turn of events, we must win. We must see if we can strike even more rapidly. This problem should be examined in depth by the General Staff.'

Towards the end of the conference, the Political Bureau still further insisted on the need to strike more rapidly. Based on a scientific analysis, it was considered that once having detected the propitious moment, it would be a crime towards our people if we were incapable of exploiting it . . .

The Political Bureau decided to mobilize to the maximum the entire resources of the Party, of the Army and the People, in both Zones and – during 1975–6 – to stimulate the military and political struggle, co-ordinated with diplomatic activity, so as to radically change the relations of force in the South in our favour . . .[4]

This is an exceptionally interesting document because it proves that even at the highest level it was not thought that victory would be possible before 1976 – a point which I was later to confirm through conversations with military and political cadres at all levels in the South. If US policy-makers were deceived about this, the Pentagon might derive some small comfort from the fact that their counterparts in Hanoi were also taken by surprise! But one of the great qualities of the Vietnamese leadership, which sometimes left even the executors of their policies breathless, was a flexibility and rapidity of decision which continually baffled the Pentagon computers. 'Two years', Le Duan had said, and at another point in his briefing, he had set the sights for the first phase of the operation – and that meant the 1975 operational season – to liberate the northern areas as far south as Danang. The whole discussion dealt with the strategic operational plans for 1975. However, not everyone at the crucial conference was convinced of the wisdom of the choice of Buon Me Thuot as the first target, and it was up to Le Duc Tho, a senior member of the Politbureau, at a meeting of the Permanent Bureau of the Central Military Committee to win them round. This he did, and the Central Military Committee, responsible for

4. Ibid, pp 32–4.

implementing the conference decisions, code-named the campaign 'Operation 275'. It was on the suggestion of Le Duan and Le Duc Tho, that Van Tien Dung was charged with the field command in the name of the Politbureau and the High Command.

Twenty-three years earlier, at the head of 320th Division, Van Tien Dung had conducted an audacious attack against the French stronghold of Phat Diem, the main centre of Catholicism in North Vietnam. In a lightning attack, he had destroyed the French headquarters and withdrawn to Vietminh positions in the outskirts with hardly any losses. Later this had been designated as a 'lotus-blossoming' operation, after the habit of lotus buds to burgeon into full bloom at dawn. He had had only fifteen days' military training before taking part in his first operations in Cao Bang province during the August 1945 uprisings, together with a short training period 'abroad' in a non-specified friendly country after the 1954 Geneva Agreement restored independence to the northern half of the country. But he remained firmly rooted in his country's, and his own, military experiences. 'Formed in action as an underground militant in an autonomous cell which had lost contact with the Party, I developed a strong feeling of independence and relying on my own initiative.' Precious qualities, indeed, for a revolutionary leader operating far afield from his headquarters! But they were the sort of qualities that Ho Chi Minh looked for when picking his key commanders. He was not one to be in search of 'yes-men', and it was no accident that Van Tien Dung's sturdy independence, in addition to his courage and natural military aptitudes, won him a founder place on the Central Military Committee. How to bring these qualities to bear in the most effective manner on the task in hand? This was the question which crowded all others from his mind. Could the 'lotus-blossoming' operation be repeated?

Buon Me Thuot, city of 150,000, was the headquarters of Saigon's 23rd Division, capital of Dac Lac province and often considered the unofficial capital of the Central Highlands, composed of the five provinces of Kontum, Gia Lai, Phu Bon, Dac Lac and Quang Duc. Before leaving Hanoi, Truong

144

Chinh, a former General Secretary of the Lao Dong Party, advised Van Tien Dung to deal mighty blows of strategic annihilation as at Dien Bien Phu. 'Two or three blows of this kind – and the enemy will collapse . . .'[5] Other farewell calls on Le Duan, Vo Nguyen Giap and Le Duc Tho had all produced the same sort of advice. But none of them knew just *how* it was to be carried out, the attack was something that Van Tien Dung had to figure out on the spot. Surprisingly, it was the image of the discreet green-sheathed lotus bud, suddenly blossoming into full bloom, that kept impinging on his consciousness! If only it could explode into life in the very heart of Buon Me Thuot! Then the idea came to him. Why not use the *dac cong* (literally, special sappers), the highly trained élite commandos, as an integral part of his forces in a co-ordinated attack.

The *dac cong* had been developed from daring groups of guerillas who had pulled off spectacular exploits, such as blowing up seventy-eight French combat and transport planes on the heavily guarded airfields of Hanoi and Haiphong at the start of the Battle of Dien Bien Phu. In the war against the Americans they had specialized in such feats as the blowing up of American officers' clubs in the heart of Saigon and sinking the aircraft carrier, *Card*, in Saigon harbour. It was a *dac cong* group that had taken over the first floor of the US Embassy in Saigon during the 1968 Tet Offensive and almost succeeded in taking over the whole embassy. Previously their actions had sometimes been co-ordinated with other operations, but not as an integral unit of an attack force. Normally they had a great deal of autonomy in deciding when and where to launch their devastating surprise raids. The idea that developed in *Tuan*'s mind as he continued south for a decisive conference with his field commanders at which battle plans had to be finalized, was to use a *dac cong* force as the 'lotus blossom', backed up by the powerful support forces which were converging on the area. In this way the crucial weapon of surprise could be wielded. As in all other operations a major consideration was to win the battle with minimum combatant casualties and human and material losses for the

5. Ibid, p 44.

145

civilian population. *Tuan* had a crushing numerical superiority which would have ensured victory in a classic frontal assault, but this was neither his 'style' nor what his superiors would have expected from him.

The forces we were committing in this campaign were our regulars from the Central Highlands, from the High Command and from the 5th Zone (the latter comprising the five northernmost provinces of South Vietnam), fairly well prepared for their mission, eager to go and with excellent morale. In general these units had been reinforced and brought up to full strength. Several of them knew the terrain very well and had a rich experience behind them. The indispensable road network had been completed and the supply situation was satisfactory. The Command Posts had been set up at all levels and were already well 'run in'.

Over the whole operational theatre we did not have overwhelming infantry superiority. But as we were able to concentrate on the main sector our superiority was undeniable: 5.5 against 1 for infantry; 1.2 against 1 for tanks and armoured cars; 2.1 against 1 for heavy artillery. There were however some weaknesses: the capability for operational converging movements was not the same in all units; we lacked experience in attacking built-up areas and, for certain units, co-ordination between the various arms on a large scale was still something new.[6]

The three main cities of the Central Highlands, Pleiku, Kontum and Buon Me Thuot, are situated in almost a straight north–south line, Kontum, the furthest north, about 40 kms from Pleiku, and Buon Me Thuot about 150 kms south of Pleiku, the three cities linked by Highway 14. Pleiku is linked with Qui Nhon on the Coastal Plains by Highway 19, and Buon Me Thuot with the port of Nha Trang, also on the Coastal Plains, by Highway 21. As the Saigon Army had been formed in the American image, with mobility assured by helicopters and air transport planes, its effectiveness had been

6. Ibid, pp 57–8.

146

severely reduced with the American departure and the resultant shortage of planes – and fuel. Its mobility, by the time *Tuan* presented his battle plan, very much depended on keeping open the three key highways, Nos. 14, 19 and 21.

The plan sounded simple, but combined the orthodox with the highly unorthodox from a text-book military viewpoint. Feint attacks at Pleiku were planned to fool the enemy into thinking that was the main target, forcing him to withdraw some of his forces from the real target. When this was done, regiment- and division-sized units would move into position along the key highways, blocking the return of the forces despatched to Pleiku and any other reinforcing units sent to Buon Me Thuot. The 'lotus flower' would blossom in the heart of the city and, together with other forces infiltrated into the city, would expand outwards, catching the defenders between 'blossomers' and the 'besiegers', who, by then, would have advanced to the city outskirts.

In reality, the plan worked. Feint attacks to the west of Pleiku sent a regiment of Saigon's 23rd Division scuttling up Highway 14 from Buon Me Thuot. Later a division-sized barricade swung into position to block their return, none other than the 320th which Van Tien Dung had commanded in innumerable actions during the anti-French war! As for what happened next, who can describe it better than *Tuan* himself.

At exactly 2 am on 10 March, by attacking the city's military airfield, the rear base of the 63rd Regiment, the civilian airport and the supply depot, our *dac cong* gave the signal for the attack. At the same time our artillery and rocket batteries opened up a deluge of fire on the headquarters of the 23rd Division, keeping it up by bursts of fire until 6.30 am, creating panic at the very nerve centre of the defence positions which were quickly paralysed. Within one hour, our *dac cong*, highly experienced and long trained by our special élite forces, were masters of the greater part of the city airport. In the twinkling of an eye, they had also occupied a corner of the Hoa Binh military airport and the whole of the Mai Hac De supply depot.

147

Taking advantage of the deafening noise of the deto-
nations; our rocket-launchers at the ready; our self-
propelled anti-aircraft guns, our tanks, armoured cars
and motorized infantry pushed ahead to the city centre
from all sides (the 316th advancing from the most difficult southern side).

Listening to the unleashing of this tempest, all of us at
the Command Post breathed a sigh of relief. The extreme
tension of deploying our troops for the assault was over.
Frankly speaking, it was not all that easy to get a battle
corps of twelve infantry regiments with their supporting
arms into position at the exact hour and minute, in that
one night, without any snags. Some units had to go ahead
secretly to take up positions in the city outskirts while
the main motorized infantry force and their supporting
armour were spread out all over the place, hidden away
and camouflaged, ready to plunge ahead towards their
assigned targets in the centre of the city.[7]

It is worth pondering over the implications of this. The
objective fact is that Saigon had no inkling that powerful
enemy forces, including tanks, artillery and motorized troops
had taken up positions within striking distance of one of their
key bases. How was this possible? Tanks made an enormous
noise; artillery pieces – including Sam 2 anti-aircraft missiles –
and truck convoys, are bulky and highly visible objects.
Someone, indeed thousands of 'someones' must have spotted
them moving into position, but the word never reached either
the Buon Me Thuot command or Saigon. That this was
possible exploded the myth that because Saigon controlled
provincial capitals it also controlled the surrounding countryside. The disintegration of Saigon prestige – partly because of
its insistence on continuing the war, partly because it relied
exclusively on repression to exert control – was such that
even its local officials heaved a sigh of relief at the régime's
impending destruction.

A second observation is that camouflage technique must be
included among the war-winning weapons of the VPA, one

7. Ibid, pp 81–2.

148

of those typical outgrowths of military confrontation between the weak and the strong, the few and the many. It was carried to the highest perfection by essentially guerilla forces waging war against an enemy which had a monopoly of air power, including a permanent 'eye in the sky', with means of calling in the bombers for every target spotted. In fact, reliance on air power implied failure to control territory and the VPA employed fantastic techniques, relying essentially on nature – local vegetation – as their friendliest ally. Of roads leading to Dien Bien Phu, which I travelled along in February/March 1954, swarming with activity at night, French spotter planes found no trace in daytime. I watched porters and local villagers planting trees and bamboo on them in the pre-dawn hours. The French had no idea that such supply routes existed, so they could not know that the VPA had encircled the Dien Bien Phu valley with artillery, until their 75s, and soon after their 105s, opened up and knocked out French artillery positions. From the first until the last day of that battle, French and American planes bombed at puffs of smoke, released by special VPA pyrotechnic units, while the real artillery continued, unmolested, to hammer key French targets, finally putting both Dien Bien Phu airstrips out of action.

How was it possible that American air power at its zenith failed to halt the north–south movement of supplies; failed to cause any damage to bridges and other communication links that could not be repaired within a maximum of four hours? I watched bamboo bridges being wound up from river beds by hand-operated winches around sun-down and lowered again just before sun-up; others assembled from beautifully camouflaged pontoon elements, hidden under overhanging bamboo thickets along the river banks. Tracks leading to these crossing points were carefully planted with vegetation during daylight hours. How many hundreds or thousands of trucks passed over those bridges during the steady twelve hours of night, year in, year out, the US Air Force, with all its infra-red photography and other gadgetry, could never know.

Villagers living within the perimeter of Buon Me Thuot might have been surprised by the noise of saws and axes at work on the night of 9–10 March, but they never reported back to the authorities what they heard or saw. In fact, tree trunks which might have offered resistance to the VPA tanks were being cut half-way through so as not to impede the pre-dawn dash towards their targets the following morning. Speed, secrecy, surprise – that this could be achieved with modern, heavy weapons is one of the miracles of which only Vietnamese revolutionary forces seem capable. Van Tien Dung spoke of all this as if it were one of the most natural of things. His written account continues:

Some of our tank units, in bivouacs 40 kms from Buon Me Thuot, surged from their hide-outs, knocking down trees that had already been sawn in half. Crushing all obstacles, they dashed at full speed past the defensive positions which dotted the roads, racing towards the city centre. Our tanks, armoured cars and self-propelled artillery crossed the Sre Pok [river which flows west and south of Buon Me Thuot] on hastily assembled ferries, despite the rapid current. The mountains and forests of the Central Highlands trembled under a deluge of exploding shells. All the columns arrived at their appointed rendezvous points at the set hour. We had scored a first point.

Gradually the sun came up. The silhouettes of enemy posts became exposed to the eyes of our artillery men. At 7.15 a.m., at an agreed signal, all our batteries concentrated their fire on the headquarters of the 23rd Division; the provincial military command and on the headquarters of their armoured units. Two of our infantry battalions which had infiltrated the city from the south during the night, occupied a number of assigned targets. Taking advantage of the results of our heavy artillery fire they quickly seized control of the main central crossroads where six streets converge and pushing ahead from there . . . occupied the eastern part of the divisional headquarters.

Supported by air cover the garrison launched a heavy counter-attack in the hope of forcing us to disengage. A violent battle ensued. At 9 a.m., our infantry, supported by tanks, attacked the Dac Lac provincial military head-quarters, which commanded all the local militia forces. As there was a very tough resistance we had to call up reserves and launch attack after attack. When at 1.30 p.m. we succeeded in forcing the gates, the garrison was still holding out in the different floors of their living quarters. After blowing up, one after another, all these centres of resistance we had completely mastered the situation by 5.30 p.m.[8]

So it went on. As it was the opening, and thus decisive, battle of the campaign and the Buon Me Thuot defenders received repeated exhortations to hold the city at all costs, it was fought out with extreme violence in a 'kill or be killed' atmosphere. The maximum of air power was thrown in by Saigon, the attackers using their 'grab the enemy by the belt' tactics to neutralize the effectiveness of Saigon's monopoly of air power and ensure that they could not be attacked without risk to the defending troops. Each air intervention was followed by infantry counter-attacks in some sectors, while *Tuan*'s men were pushing ahead at top speed in others. From the south-west, a column of tank-supported infantry rushed through the Mai Hac De supply centre, already in the hands of the *dac cong*, to seize the radio communications centre and thus threaten the key prize – the headquarters of the 23rd Division from the west. By the end of the first day, virtually the whole city was in VPA hands, except the divisional head-quarters which was obviously situated in the most securely defendable position. Eighty air attacks had not been able to halt the forward thrust from all sides, and the defenders had withdrawn block by block, building by building towards the divisional headquarters.

It was only by the end of that first day of unremitting violent combat that Saigon realized Buon Me Thuot was *it*, and a major error of judgement had been made. But it was too late. Especially as there was no possibility of airlifting troops from Pleiku to the rescue. Apart from lack of transport planes, *Tuan*'s artillery was already pounding the Pleiku airstrip.

8. Ibid, pp 82–3.

And a large section of Highway 14 was very solidly in the hands of the 320th VPA Division. The end was not long in coming, and by 10.30 am on 11 March the city had fallen.

On that same morning *Tuan* sent the message that every field commander dreams of sending and every overall commander dreams of receiving. As the lotus flower continued to unfold in every direction along the roads leading out of the city, Vo Nguyen Giap received the following telegram:

> To Comrade *Chien*. We are the complete masters of Buon Me Thuot. We have occupied all major targets, the Headquarters of the 23rd Division, the Dac Lac provincial military headquarters, the tank and armoured car park and the city airport. We are pursuing fleeing troops within the city. First reports are of about one thousand prisoners and important booty . . . We have captured a dozen artillery pieces and almost one hundred tons of shells . . . This day, 11 March, the Military Administrative Committee of Dac Lac province takes over and I propose to promote Y Blok[9] to colonel and make him Chairman of this Committee.[10]

Tuan further proposed, among other plans, that he follow up the Buon Me Thuot success by taking Pleiku, isolating Kontum, leaving a push to the south until a little later.

---

9. Y. Blok, when the author first met him, towards the end of 1963, was the head of a company of Montagnard tribespeople carrying out guerilla activities in the outskirts of Buon Me Thuot. His company had been expanded into a regiment and he had risen to the rank of lieutenant-colonel at the time of the Buon Me Thuot battle.

10. *Dai Thang Mua Xuan*, op cit, pp 88–9.

CHAPTER 13

THIEU PANICS

The role of the *dac cong*, and the speed with which everything happened, caused great panic at President Nguyen Van Thieu's headquarters. Even the normally well informed were confused as to what had taken place. Communiqués from Saigon continued to claim that Buon Me Thuot was still in Saigon hands. Paul Léandri, the very competent and courageous Saigon correspondent of *Agence France Presse*, was shot dead as he stalked out of the Saigon police headquarters, for refusing to reveal the source of his cable to the effect that the city had fallen, not to the North Vietnamese, but to local Montagnard tribespeople. Tank-supported troops had only moved in after local troops started to suppress the Montagnards. Léandri was shot three days after the city had been taken. Four days later, on 18 March, Father Tran Tuu Thanh, who headed the People's Anti-Corruption Movement in Saigon, held a press conference to affirm that the first troops to enter Buon Me Thuot were several thousand FULRO[1]

1. FULRO (United Front for the Struggle of the Oppressed Races) had originally been set up by the French to try to win back some influence in the Central Highlands. Later it was taken over by the CIA, betrayed, and many of its members slaughtered when Saigon applied pressure to have the Montagnards totally under their own control. Paul Léandri, Father Tran Tuu Thanh and myself (in my book *Grasshoppers and Elephants*, New York, 1977) were mistaken. Van Tien Dung's account makes it clear that what appeared to be an internal uprising was the well-planned infiltration of the *dac cong*, whose speciality from that time on was to act as the vanguard of the attacking force, but always disguised as something else.

Montagnards, supported by local residents. Troops moved in only after the city had practically been taken over by the local population.

Father Tran maintained that if the city had fallen so rapidly this was because of Saigon's repressive policy towards the Montagnards. In fact, because this was the opening blow of the campaign, the local people's organizations had not been tipped off – for security reasons – to surface and play their part. As distinct from the case of every other of the forty-two capitals captured during the whirlwind campaign, the role of the local people in Buon Me Thuot was not all that important. It was a case of concentrating overwhelming superiority of force on a selected target and, above all, exploiting the element of surprise – especially the ace card of the *dac cong*. This was a card to be played over and over again in the weeks that followed, and it is doubtful if the Saigon Command realized, at any point during the war, the exact extent and scope of their activities. Indeed, there was so much treachery and desertion from the Saigon ranks that the sudden appearance of troops in Saigon uniform, seizing a bridge or blowing one up, would be written off as another case of desertion. In fact, it would be a *dac cong* unit performing an assigned task.

When I asked Van Tien Dung what were his main problems in preparing the battle, he replied that a major problem was that of guarding absolute secrecy. As an example, he said that a battalion of the 320th Division had ambushed an enemy artillery unit speeding down Highway 14, towards Buon Me Thuot. It was from Saigon's 45th Regiment and the divisional commander concluded that the 45th was being sent to reinforce Buon Me Thuot. He asked permission to block Highway 14 and wipe out the regiment. 'I had to send a stern reply to the effect that the 320th must remain "dead" and no activities must be carried out on Highway 14 without my express orders.' Another anxious moment was when one of his own artillerymen was wounded in a surprise clash and it was known that like so many VPA soldiers he carried a diary. It was learned that he had been taken to hospital, where his leg was amputated, and that the Saigon 23rd divisional

154

commander considered his capture so important that he was waiting for the artilleryman to recover consciousness to interrogate him personally. 'In fact our men snatched him from the hospital and returned him to his unit before the interrogation could take place.'

The murder of Paul Léandri was a measure of the concern at the Saigon Command Headquarters at the realization that Buon Me Thuot had irrevocably fallen. And if no decision at all was taken following the loss of the provincial capital of Phuoc Binh two months earlier, a speedy and disastrous decision was taken over the loss of Buon Me Thuot. Orders to retake the city 'at all costs' were as absurd as those 'to hold it at all costs'. Forty-eight hours before the attack was launched, the 320th Division moved astride Highway 14, completing the isolation of the city.

On the afternoon of 12 March *Tuan* received a cable from *Chien* congratulating him on behalf of the Politbureau and the Central Military Committee for the 'brilliant victory', unreservedly approving plans for pushing ahead to seize Pleiku and isolating Kontum, which could be dealt with

A few minutes later we got another telegram from the High Command informing us that according to the latest news the enemy counted on retaking Buon Me Thuot, relying on their air power and by throwing into a counter-offensive everything they had left [in the 2nd Tactical Zone], elements of the 53rd Regiment, the 21st Rangers Group, garrisons from neighbouring towns such as Buon Ho and Phuoc An [150 kms north of Buon Me Thuot on Highway 14, and 30 kms east on Highway 21 respectively], together with reinforcements of a regiment or two of Regulars and Rangers. Other intelligence reports warned that the 45th Regiment, and the field headquarters of the 23rd Division[2] had left Pleiku by helicopter for Buon Ho at midday of 11 March, and that another headquarters group was expected at Phuoc An the following

2. The 23rd Division comprised the 53rd, 44th and 45th Regiments, together with supporting tank and artillery units.

day. The enemy air force was extremely active. For us the most urgent task now was to concentrate our forces to wipe out as quickly as possible all enemy units and bases around Buon Me Thuot and crush all reinforcements.

Those two telegrams rejoiced our hearts. Full of enthusiasm for our successes and sure of others ahead, we started to tackle them.[3]

One of *Tuan*'s first worries was the classical one of any field-commander in any war. How are my supplies? An enormous quantity had been used up in the main operation. In most of Van Tien Dung's campaign experiences till then – as in those of Vo Nguyen Giap – logistics had to be reckoned in terms of supplies that could be carried on the backs of men and women, strapped to the sides of bicycle frames or stacked on the bottoms of ox-drawn carts. Those packed into trucks – whether made in Moscow or Shanghai – were a recent luxury. However, his worries were unfounded, and in discussion with his logistics chief, Dinh Duc Thien, he discovered that the vehicle parks and munitions depots were well stocked.

The Saigon counter-attacks were disastrous failures. As had been expected, the 45th Regiment had been helicoptered from Pleiku to Phuoc An on 12 March, and on the same day Thieu had cabled the commander of the 23rd Division 'to hold Buon Me Thuot at all costs'. At about the time he should have received that cable, the captured 23rd Division commander was giving some highly valuable information to Van Tien Dung's secretary!

It was not only enemy counter-attacks and their air activities that *Tuan* had to cope with.

At our headquarters, the map was starred with circles cancelled out with red crosses to indicate positions taken by our forces, with red arrows indicating the directions of our advance and blue arrows indicating the enemy's retreat towards the surrounding forests.

3. *Dai Thang Mua Xuan*, op cit, pp 96–7.

At midday on 12 March, at the most critical moment – in the heat of the enemy's counter-attack – all our telephones suddenly went dead. No sound of bombs, no drone of aircraft! Also no response to our calls. We stopped everything, looking at each other and shaking our heads. At the very moment that one of the comrades responsible for communications dashed out of the bunker to find out what had happened, we heard the trumpeting of a herd of elephants about 300 metres away.

Terrified by the roar of battle, they were 'retreating' in their own manner, heading for the Cambodian frontier by the shortest route which happened to cut straight across our headquarters area. The lines were not just broken, but simply torn out for long stretches.[4]

Despite this temporary interruption in communications, for Van Tien Dung and his troops the victory over the Saigon troops was relatively easy. Using their own and abandoned enemy transport the VPA troops bypassed the fleeing troops, set up road-blocks ahead of them and either wiped them out or captured them in full flight. Thieu's aircraft circled overhead, impotent to intervene with the hopeless intermingling of forces from both sides and ground–air communications non-existent. By dawn of the 14th, the day on which Léandri was shot for having reported the fall of Buon Me Thuot and his version of how and why, Van Tien Dung said he received a summing-up report to the effect that the three regiments of the 23rd Division, plus the 21st Rangers Group had been entirely wiped out. The 2nd Army Corps, responsible for the defence of the 2nd Tactical Military Region, had been wiped out and, as *Tuan* cabled to *Chien* on the evening of that day: 'We pledge ourselves to do everything possible to fulfil the tasks assigned to us, achieving in the Central Highlands in the first quarter of 1975, the victories planned for the following year.'[5]

The most complete confirmation of the brilliance of the

4. Ibid, pp 103–4.
5. Ibid, pp 105–7.

decision to strike at Buon Me Thuot by Hanoi's military–political leadership came with Nguyen Van Thieu's decision on 14 March to abandon Pleiku, Kontum and virtually the whole of the 2nd Military Zone. Militarily speaking, Thieu was no fool and sometimes could read the signals better than his American advisers. With the loss of Buon Me Thuot and the destruction of the most of the best that he had in the Central Highlands, his next best move was to secure the Coastal Plains which, among other things, sheltered the main north–south communications route, strategic Highway 1. Orders were given to all remaining forces in Zone 2, to head for the coast. They never made it. Road-blocks had been in place for a whole week in anticipation of just that. VPA units, released by the Buon Me Thuot victory, dashed in all directions through forests and grasslands to secure all possible access routes to the Coastal Plains. Local units joined in, occupying bridges and mountain passes. Enormous traffic jams built up, panic feeding on panic, helped inadvertently by Saigon's psychological warfare services, which urged local populations to flee advancing 'Communist hordes', because if they stayed they would be wiped out as 'pro-Communist sympathizers' in the victorious counter-attack which would inevitably follow.

While President and Commander-in-Chief Nguyen Van Thieu was exhorting the 23rd Division to hold – or at least recapture – Buon Me Thuot what was the Divisional Commander Colonel Vu The Quang telling Major Mac Lam, *Tuan*'s most experienced interrogating officer? Like virtually every other high-ranking Saigon officer captured, Vu The Quang was very co-operative. No banging his head on the ground to cut off his tongue as Ho Chi Minh's ancestor had done!

Your attack on Buon Me Thuot was completely unforeseen by our High Command and even by the Americans. After Phuoc Long our evaluation was that you could attack some small towns, like An Loc or Gia Nghia, but that big urban centres such as Buon Me Thuot, Pleiku or Tay Tinh were beyond your capacity. When you attacked

158

Buon Me Thuot, we thought that was only a diversionary attack and that the real target was Gia Nghia [an important communications centre, 75 kms south-west of Buon Me Thuot and about 15kms from the Cambodian border.][6]

The colonel went on to describe the pitiful situation of the Saigon forces in the rest of the 2nd Corps area, pointing out that the 3rd Division, supposedly one of Saigon's best, was only at half strength and it would take three months to build it up to full strength. He pointed out that the situation was very favourable for the VPA to push on down to the Coastal Plains and attack Nha Trang, at the coastal end of Highway 21. 'You only have to watch out for the naval artillery, mainly 76 mm and a few 122 mm pieces. Planes can operate rather easily there but their possibilities are limited. The F5s [Phantoms] can only make thirty sorties a day over the whole of the South. For other air attacks they have to make do with A-37s. At Nha Trang, supply by sea helps out a bit, but morale is very low and defences very disorganized. Saigon can only count on the "Marines" and Parachutists, but the latter are also very demoralized. If the "paras" or the "Marines" suffer heavy losses, the morale of the whole of the rest of the armed forces will collapse.'[7]

This was very precious information to check out against what was already known from other sources. There was more to come, because Vu The Quang had been military governor of Cam Ranh, the natural harbour-city which had been the object of an investment of hundreds of millions of dollars by the USA to transform it into the greatest naval base in the whole South China sea area. What about the defences *there*? 'No defences at all', he replied. 'It's all a great bluff. Everything built by the army faces the sea in order to have fresh air. With your methods you'll take it all over in five seconds flat. For Cam Ranh to really organize its defences would take three months. Not sure even then because they lack everything. Since the Americans left they're short of

6 and 7. Ibid, pp 88–9.

everything, sandbags, barbed wire, cement, motor transport – everything. The whole thing could collapse at any moment.'[8]

It is interesting that this information was in Van Tien Dung's hands on the night of 10 March, and was partly the basis for his optimistic telegram to Vo Nguyen Giap the following morning. But there was one thing which worried *Tuan*, and that was the lack of reliable information on the state of Highway 7, which led south-east from Pleiku to the coastal city of Tuy Hoa. Before the assault on Buon Me Thuot, he had several times asked Kim Tuan, the commander of the 320th Division, about the state of Highway 7. Each time the reply was that it had been out of action for a long time, simply because the bridges were in ruins and there were no ferries. Two days before the assault on Buon Me Thuot, he had repeated the question and received the same reply.

> Then I learned that the enemy was going to flee by this route. Our division in charge of this area had no real knowledge of its exact course and had done nothing to intercept the runaways. I was very tough with the responsible commander, twice repeating: 'This is an intolerable negligence and oversight. As things stand at this moment, the slightest hesitation, the slightest negligence, the slightest fear in the face of difficulties, the slightest delay – and all is lost. If the enemy succeeds in getting away, you will bear the entire responsibility.'
>
> In such a situation I could not tolerate anyone at a lower level evading his instructions. I counted on everyone entirely performing his duties with the maximum of responsibility. Together we had taken part in numerous battles, numerous campaigns, more than once we had been together in critical situations. But as commander, I am very strict with my comrades and they understand the reason for this. Once the order is given, they do everything to execute it – and in most cases, they succeed.

8. Ibid, p. 89.

In replacing the receiver, I saw before my eyes all the enemy retreats of which I had been witness during our resistance wars against France, later the United States.[9]

As to what Thieu was really doing and thinking, in contrast to the optimistic communiqués which continued to pour out of Saigon, there was a revealing account by Colonel Pham Duy Tat, who commanded all six Ranger Groups in the 2nd Military Region. They had all been wiped out, together with three tank regiments and the colonel-commander had been captured. He described a meeting between President Thieu, Premier General Tran Thien Khiem, Thieu's chief of staff, General Cao Van Vien, his security chief, General Dang Van Quang and the Commander of 2nd Corps, General Pham Van Phu. In reply to Thieu's question to Dang Van Quang as to how long he could hold Pleiku, without reinforcements, the general replied: 'One month provided I receive maximum air support and obtain by air everything I need – arms, munitions and men to replace the heavy losses of the last few days.' Thieu said there was no such possibility and decided on the immediate evacuation of Pleiku and Kontum. He also decided that the provincial chiefs should not be warned of the evacuation but should remain 'to organize resistance'. As for the Montagnard regional troops: 'Let them go back to their mountains', said Thieu, according to Pham Duy Tat.[10]

The so-called 'planned withdrawal' of the Saigon forces was well described at the time. It was a complete débacle. Once the high-ranking officers left with their families for Danang and cities in the Coastal Plains, the junior officers and Saigon officials and their families joined in the general flight. Plans for an orderly retreat with priorities for élite units

9. Ibid, pp 117–18. This is a rare glimpse, at such a level, of the iron discipline that was expected on the battlefield in the VPA. Although Van Tien Dung does not mention it, he must also have had in mind the fury of Vo Nguyen Giap, when a commander of the southern front at Dien Bien Phu – in a similar case of negligence – almost allowed a sizeable force of French troops to make their escape to Laos. Only a very tough order by Giap, and an almost super-human belated effort by the commander and his troops, rectified the error, cut the escape and ended in the interception of the fleeing troops.
10. Ibid, p 122.

and essential weapons, went by the board. There were inter-unit fights for control of Pleiku airport and for seats in whatever planes succeeded in landing. There were fights for every bridge and crossroads, and for priority on Highway 7 and every track leading from it. Small trucks pushed small cars off the road; big trucks did the same with small trucks; tanks crushed big trucks under their tracks if they did not make way in time. 'Making way' along the road often meant plunging down a precipice with a slender chance of a stout tree preventing too many somersaults. Plans to establish a defence line with armoured units and artillery between Pleiku and the coast went overboard with the tanks and cannon, as VPA units moved eastwards from Buon Me Thuot and westwards from the Coastal Plains, and as local guerilla units sprang into action everywhere along the line of retreat. Saigon's regional and local troops dissolved, deserted or changed sides as the dimensions of the catastrophic defeat in the Central Highlands became known.

'Changing sides' was also an important element in the situation. Tanks, armoured cars, trucks, artillery pieces were captured in great quantities. But who were to drive them and aim them competently? The VPA had prepared some specialists in this field, but not nearly enough to cope with the vast weight of material that was falling into *Tuan*'s hands every hour from 12 March onwards. Why not use the American- and Saigon-trained drivers and artillery experts? From the battle of Buon Me Thuot onwards this was done to an ever-increasing degree. Some did it from conviction, some from opportunism – to be on the winning side – others perhaps from pressure to 'redeem' themselves. But in *Tuan*'s view the possibility of using the other side's specialists was not fully or quickly enough exploited. He was a worker, with the quick reactions of one dealing with spindles and shuttles. But he was in charge of an army of soldiers and officers whose reactions were those of men dealing with ploughs and oxen. Despite all their battlefield experience, it often came down to that. Doubtless it was the rapid reflexes of an industrial worker that Ho Chi Minh considered necessary to inject into the military leadership of an essentially peasant and intellectual-led revolution, when he included Van Tien Dung in the Central Military Committee.

Despite the great victory, which was decisive for everything that was to follow, *Tuan* was not completely satisfied. He recognized that Thieu had panicked and 'from a tactical mistake at the operational level, Thieu had slipped into a strategic error, and that any strategic error eventually leads to the loss of a war'.[11] He was satisfied that by the surprise blow at Buon Me Thuot, Thieu had been led into committing the supreme mistake of evacuating the Central Highlands. But, wrote *Tuan*:

> There were weaknesses on our side that had to be overcome without delay. Sometimes lack of nerve, at others the routine of old operational methods . . . At all levels conceptions were out-dated in relation to the new conditions. The weight of old habits still made itself felt. Too many interminable meetings and discussions without anyone coming forward with swift decisions or speedy execution of decisions already taken. In some cases our troops were not sufficiently disciplined. And instead of using captured field radios, telephone lines were being endlessly unwound.[12]

Tuan clearly saw the importance of finding time to teach the armed forces – even between battles – to react with flexibility and maximum mobility, and to utilize to the full captured enemy vehicles, arms and techniques. And he did this.

Thus it was that in future battles there were not only *dac cong* in Saigon uniforms, but also American tanks and self-propelled guns; and American armoured cars and General Motors trucks, hurtling along the roads of the VPA's advance.

If the battle for Buon Me Thuot has been described in some detail, it is because it was crucial to everything else that happened. It started the process of confusion and demoralization which dominated the thinking and decisions of the Saigon Command and its American advisers from that

11. Ibid, p 124.
12. Ibid, p 109.

163

moment on. Whatever they did subsequently was wrong because they lost any capacity for initiative they ever had. The propaganda machine could continue to turn out comforting communiqués, but officers and men had a more realistic view as to the dimensions of the defeat in the initial loss of Buon Me Thuot; the still more staggering defeat in the attempts to retake it; and the final disaster of the attempted evacuation of the Central Highlands.

What next? Saigon still had enormous military forces at its disposal. Military Zones 1, 3 and 4 and the Special Zone around Saigon were still intact. One of the panic measures taken by President Nguyen Van Thieu – obviously thinking of his own skin rather than how military historians would assess his handling of the campaign – was to withdraw the 1st Airborne Division from just south of the demarcation line along the Seventeenth Parallel to reinforce the defences of Saigon. It was one of his best divisions, and *Chien* and *Tuan* noted its departure with considerable interest. Thieu had become worried by mutterings in his entourage about errors in judging the adversary's intentions; his indecision over Phuoc Long; his wrong decision to pull out of the Central Highlands. The risk of a coup to replace him was as much in his mind as the risk of a sudden swing south by the VPA, when he transferred the 1st Airborne from Quang Tri to the Saigon area. A sudden upsurge of guerilla activity in the Mekong delta to the south and in Tay Ninh province just to the north of Saigon contributed to what had clearly become a panic atmosphere at Thieu's headquarters. He started issuing orders which his field commanders had neither the intention, nor the possibility, of obeying.

CHAPTER 14

PEOPLE'S WAR

The official title of the operation that Giap and Dung were directing was 'The 1975 Spring General Offensive and People's Uprisings', and it was no misnomer. If the people's role was not so apparent in that critical first knock-out blow because of the reason explained earlier, it was crucial in every operation that followed. It could not be otherwise because it was central to all the teachings of 'Uncle Ho' and his teachings were sacrosanct for *Chien* and *Tuan* and those they commanded. Everything done, everything said, had to be acceptable to the ordinary people, the peasants from the rice-growing plains to the tribal hunters in the highlands.

Events moved swiftly after the collapse in the Central Highlands and the débâcle of the attempted withdrawal to the Coastal Plains. People's organizations, which had survived wave after wave of extermination campaigns, such as the CIA's Phoenix Program aimed at assassinating all suspected Vietcong members and sympathizers, surfaced to operate as battle-hardened auxiliaries to the VPA regular and regional forces as they started to sweep aside provincial and district strongholds of the Saigon forces. Encirclement of the latter's bases reached strangulation point. Propaganda teams, including wives and mothers of the besieged troops, intensified their efforts, urging them to surrender or turn their guns on their officers, while there was still time. The simple precept of siding with the 'troops of the just cause' was a constant theme of the propaganda teams, operating from zig-zagging trench systems which crept ever closer to the Saigon positions. Word of the shattering defeat in the Central Highlands lent greater weight than ever to their simple arguments and homely language.

And there was no let-up of military action, especially in the 1st Military Zone which included the prestigious former imperial capital of Hue, and the great aero-naval base of Danang. Quang Tri, capital of the northernmost province of the same name, fell without a fight – he t roops taking the advice of the propaganda teams, either going back to their villages or joining the 'troops of the just cause'. Within a few days of the fall of Buon Me Thuot, and before the battle to crush the counter-attacks and cut off the fleeing survivors was over, *Tuan* had sent some of his crack troops speeding north-east to cut the Hue–Danang road and open a new front in the 1st Military Zone, or what Hanoi designated as the Tri Thien (Quang Tri–Thua Thien) region. The 2nd Army Corps accordingly went into action to the south-west of Hue, along the Nui Bong–Nui Nghe line, and, by repelling counter-attacks and pinning down mobile forces, they prevented the Saigon forces withdrawing in the Tri Thien area. In the plains, seven battalions of the regional forces and a hundred *dac cong* groups carried out an in-depth penetration. And with the support of guerilla forces and the local population, they simultaneously opened fire in eight districts, seized the district centre of Mai Linh, wiped out eleven of the thirty local military posts and carried out armed propaganda in fifty-three villages which had a total of over 20,000 inhabitants.

This was typical of what was happening all over the country following the firing of the signal shot at Buon Me Thuot. But such actions were now openly part of the main thrust of The General Offensive and People's Uprisings. The whole of Quang Tri province was liberated, essentially by people's uprisings, by 19 March. A factor overlooked in the world press – and this is not a criticism of the working journalists, many of whom repeatedly risked their lives, some losing them, to obtain the real facts – is that most of South Vietnam had been 'lost' long before The 1975 Spring Offensive started. There is no explanation for the fact that the loss of a provincial capital was synonymous with the loss of an entire province other than that the province had been 'lost' for years, the capital being often the only bit of real estate still held by the Saigon régime. A very expensive propaganda machine in Washington and Saigon, however, perpetuated the myth that because Thieu controlled provincial capitals he controlled the country. It took a few taps on the head of those capitals to prove the contrary! There is no other explanation for the fact that forty-three provinces, together with their capitals, 'fell' within fifty-five days from the time *Chien-Tuan* opened their offensive! The Saigon generals were excellent at making eloquent statements of intent to defend those capitals, *Chien's* and *Tuan's* generals were excellent at capturing them! While the Saigon troops were fleeing from Quang Tri, eventually to establish a defence line along the My Chanh river just north of Hue, General Ngo Quang Truong, entrusted with the defence of the whole 1st Corps area, broadcast over Hue radio: 'I will die in the city streets. Only over my body will the Vietcong march into the streets of our ancient capital.'

Two days later, Hue was encircled and six days later, General Ngo Quang Truong having fled the scene, Hue was taken. The VPA entered the city from several directions simultaneously, guided to their targets by local people's organizations, who by this time were out in full strength. *Tuan* records that he learned of the liberation of Hue in his headquarters bunker on the afternoon of 26 March. 'I lit a cigarette. I had stopped smoking long ago, but whenever some thorny problem was settled or we had scored some important victory; whenever some success took a heavy weight off my shoulders, I smoked a fag to mark the occasion.'[1]

The victory at Hue opened the way to Danang. Thieu had gone on the air at Saigon to say: 'We withdrew from Kontum and Pleiku in order to conserve intact our forces. But Danang, Hue and the 3rd and 4th Military Zones, however, will be

1. Ibid, p 130.

defended to the death.' But he could not persuade his generals, far less his captains and troops, of the necessity for this!

On the same day that Hue fell – part of its garrison being evacuated by sea to Danang – the capitals of two provinces further south, Tam Ky, capital of Danang province, and Quang Ngai, capital of the province of the same name, were liberated entirely by people's uprisings. The garrisons simply packed up, fled or changed sides when red flags suddenly appeared on all public buildings and garrison headquarters.

According to the precise information reaching *Chien* in Hanoi, Thieu and his US advisers in Saigon absolutely discounted the idea that there was any imminent danger to Danang. It would take at least a month or two for Giap to digest the enormous gains in the Central Highlands and the Tri–Thien northern sectors. In any text-book type of military operations this would have been correct. It would have been correct in the case of the Saigon Army pushing north into Hanoi's territory. A whole military occupation administration would have to be set up and a large part of the operational forces tied down in 'mopping-up' operations to bring the occupied areas under control. But one of the great advantages of 'People's War' was that all these tasks, including looking after their own and enemy wounded, transport, supplies and administration, were handled by the local people's organizations. Thus the fighting forces could concentrate on the job of fighting and moving from one job to another with the minimum of delay.

Thieu and his American advisers had intended to promote an enormous north–south movement of refugees, by the old trick of twenty years earlier when the French, acting on the advice of US psychological warfare experts, had threatened Catholics with atomic fire unless they 'followed the Virgin Mary' to the South. Dramatic calls were launched for international shipping to converge on Danang to save refugees fleeing from 'Vietcong terror'. In fact, by carefully scanning western press accounts, it was clear that many were fleeing the destruction-bombing of towns abandoned by Saigon and the wave of pillage and rape by the retreating Saigon troops. The calls fell mainly on deaf ears and the speed of developments frustrated the Saigon–Washington plan to gain time by this means. However *Tuan* was urged to act still faster. The day after the fall of Hue, *Chien* cabled him to 'exploit the situation to the maximum, maximum speed, maximum surprise', and to act in a spirit of 'absolute certainty of victory'. He was ordered to 'act with audacity to achieve surprise and not give the enemy time to react'; to concentrate his forces to crush the enemy garrison at Danang, essentially the 3rd Infantry Division and the Marine Division.[2]

What happened next was an illustration of the speed and flexibility with which Hanoi could react to new situations, and the rapidity with which decisions at the top were translated into action on the battlefield. No trace of ox and plough mentality in what happened on 25 March! A special command was set up to direct the battle for Danang, headed by General Le Trong Tan who was rushed down from Hanoi for the job, with General Chu Huy Man as his political commissar. Three divisions, the 304th, 324th and 325th, were ordered to converge on Danang, sending their heavy artillery in advance to pound the airfield and port areas. *Tuan* remained in overall command and gave instructions for an intensification of military activities to prevent further enemy reinforcement of the Danang area. The movement of the three crack VPA divisions could not be kept secret, nor the implications of the stepped-up activities of the 'persuasion' teams.

From March 25, the most complete confusion reigned in Danang. As our forces were rapidly approaching to apply pressure on the city, the enemy had to abandon his plans (to convert Danang into an impregnable fortress) and started to use Boeing 727s and helicopters to evacuate the American advisers, and part of the troops. Competition for plane seats degenerated into hand-to-hand fighting on the airfield. People were crushed under planes taking off from the air-strips; others fled by hanging on to the landing skids of helicopters. Soldiers and officers, trying to flee with their families, had fist fights trying to get aboard the planes. Before their own panic-stricken

2. Ibid, p 133.

flight, the Marines, who had looted and raped their way through the city, turned their M-16s on each other. Three thousand two hundred recruits at the Hoa Cam training centre mutinied, some to join our forces, others to return to their families. Our long-range artillery started to shell the Danang airfield, the 3rd Division Headquarters at Hoa Khanh, the Son Tra port area and the headquarters of the Marines at Non Nuoc and this obviously added to the general panic. Our comrades imprisoned at Non Nuoc rose up, sacked the prison and fled. The 2nd Division from the 5th Zone, commanded by Army hero Colonel Nguyen Chon – who had liberated Tien Phuoc, Phuoc Lam and Tam Ky, attacked Danang from the south.

On 29th March, the tank-supported infantry of the 2nd Corps [the three divisions mentioned above] supported by the [regional] forces of the 5th Zone advanced on the city from the north, the north-west, south-west and south, pressing straight on to the centre, occupying the airport and other important positions including the Son Tra peninsula. At the same time an autonomous regiment from the 5th Zone took over Non Nuoc and the Nuoc Man air base. Some of our underground comrades, together with our commandos, occupied the Trinh Minh The bridge and hoisted our flag over the Town Hall. Guided by self-defence guerillas and local inhabitants, our regular forces were rapidly masters of the key positions and started hunting down the fleeing remnants. In thirty-two hours we had crushed, or put to flight, the one hundred thousand troops massed to defend this city; we had seized a powerful military complex and liberated the second most important city in the South. The 1st Army Corps being definitely wiped off the map and even that of the puppet's 1st Tactical Zone, conditions were ripe to push the Saigon army to its total collapse.[3]

The gallant General Ngo Quang Truong, having fled from

3. Ibid, pp 134–5.

170

Hue to Danang without waiting for the Vietcong to march over his body, fled by helicopter from Danang before battle was really joined. No longer with an Army Corps or Tactical Zone to command, he sought the comfort of a 'soft and warm bed' in Saigon's Cong Hoa military hospital!

Thus was won the second most decisive battle. The victory was all the more remarkable because it had not been originally anticipated by either side. Danang was a gigantic aero-naval-army military complex. The first American estimate – and it was obviously a great under-estimate by what I saw even on the airfield, months after the débâcle – was that 300 million dollars' worth of military equipment had fallen into VPA hands during those thirty-two hours. Of the several hundred planes there was a number of Boeing 727 transports which now serve Vietnam's civilian aviation, also 200 tanks and 10,000 other military vehicles. As *Tuan* correctly commented, with two of the adversary's four Tactical Zones and the armed forces defending them wiped off the military map, the 'relation of military forces had tilted irrevocably in our favour'.[4] The point was not lost on Hanoi!

While *Tuan* was still cogitating on the dimensions of the Danang victory, he received an electrifying cable from Le Duan announcing that it had been decided to scrap previous time-tables and push straight ahead for the liberation of Saigon – and end the war. Veteran Le Duc Tho would get back into battledress and leave Hanoi on 28 March to bring detailed instructions. Other heavyweights such as Pham Hung, Tran Van Tra, Vo Chi Cong and Chu Huy Man, would meet with him to discuss the details of the next campaign. Pham Van Dong was presiding over a newly formed Support Committee to ensure the South got everything it needed. All this was contained in a cabled summary of an historic session of the Politbureau, the essence of which said:

Thus . . . we are in a position to liberate Saigon during the current dry season because we have still two months before the rains start. Once we reach the outskirts of the

4. Ibid, p 136.

city the rains will not worry us too much. We must overcome all difficulties, cost what it may. The situation is
very fluid and can still produce unpredictable changes . . .
The evolution can be swift . . . There is a qualitative
change in the situation. The decisive thing is to create the
occasion and exploit it.[5]

Le Duc Tho, that splendid successor to Nguyen Trai, the
fifteenth-century poet-diplomat-philosopher-strategist found
time on his first stop at Dong Hoi to dedicate a poem to Le
Duan:

Your last advice 'Return only as the victor.'
What to say? There are moments when words fail.
I hear the whole country through your words.
A thousand leagues through the Truong Son are as
nothing,
The road to the front resounds with only excellent news.
Everywhere joyous shouts of Victory,
Speed me on my way.
The Great Moment is knocking at the door.[6]

On 31 March, a further urgent cable had arrived from Le
Duan: 'Speed is more important than ever. Do not lose a
single moment. *Tuan* must leave immediately for the *Nam Bo*
to meet *Bay Coung* (Pham Hung). *Sau* (Le Duc Tho) is leaving
to join them there. *Bay Coung* and *Tu Nguyen* (General Tran
Van Tra) will no longer proceed to the Central Highlands.'
The 'Nam Bo' in this case meant the Provisional Revolutionary
Government's headquarters at Loc Ninh, a little over 100 kms
due north of Saigon, where *Tuan* was to establish his forward
headquarters and where some of the cream of Vietnam's
revolutionary leadership was to be concentrated.

The 1975–6 time-table was compressed into the remaining
weeks of the 1975 dry season. No wonder that Washington and
Saigon were taken by surprise. Acting on the new orders of
Le Duan and Giap, Van Tien Dung rearranged his divisions,

5. Ibid, p 148.
6. Ibid, p 159.

and redirected his military thinking to the problem of pressing right on to Saigon. This included the creation of a new 3rd Army Corps, comprising the 320th, 316th and 10th Divisions.

In four visits to the liberated zones of South Vietnam, even as far back as 1963-6, I had been astonished at the expansion of companies with ill-assorted weapons and nondescript uniforms into battalions, then regiments and finally – within three years – into divisions, with standardized weapons captured from the enemy and uniforms made in their own jungle tailoring shops. Nine years later, it was not surprising that the 'great rear' in the North had supplied them with more and better of everything, and the 'greater rear' still further back in China and the Soviet Union had supplied them with more sophisticated weapons. They had SAMs to shoot down planes, amphibian craft to cross rivers, and even multiple rocket launchers to bombard enemy artillery positions. 'Nothing succeeds like success', is as true within the Communist world as elsewhere, and Giap's version of 'People's War' had been very successful. (It was none other than the Chinese Prime Minister, Chou En-lai, who drew me aside at a Djakarta reception – to celebrate the tenth anniversary of the Bandung Conference[7] – to express his unbounded admiration for Vietnam's original development of 'People's War'. Ten years later this was approaching its fullest expression.)

That Washington had got a whiff of the crucial importance of what was going on was clear when, in late March, President Ford sent his Chief-of-Staff, General Frederick Weyand – a former Commander-in-Chief of US forces in South Vietnam – to give the western world's best professional military advice. And the advice he gave, to hold Saigon at all costs until the rainy season blocked further VPA advances, was no doubt

7. Held in May 1955, at Bandung, Indonesia, this conference was attended by heads of state and governments from countries of Asia and Africa. Premiers Chou En-lai of China and Jawaharlal Nehru of India played the leading roles. The Conference adopted the famous 'Five Principles of Peaceful Coexistence', formulated by Chou En-lai and Nehru as a guideline to relations between countries despite differing social systems during a visit by Chou En-lai to Delhi in July 1954.

sound. During the five or six months of the rainy season the Americans would undertake diplomatic initiatives to save what could be saved and under this diplomatic umbrella the South Vietnamese forces could be prepared for a counter-offensive to recover essential positions lost. After touring the frontline areas with a coterie of US military specialists and Thieu's Chief-of-Staff, General Weyand recommended an outer defence line anchored on Phan Rang, about 300 kms north-east of Saigon, on the Coastal Plains. It would run through to the Central Highlands to block any VPA advance to Saigon along Highway 1 – the most obvious approach route. In case this was breached, an inner defence line should be set up, anchored on Xuan Loc, capital of Long Khanh province, about 60 kms north-east of Saigon and 30 kms from the huge Bien Hoa air base. It was at Xuan Loc that the third great battle was to take place. Weyand was correct in insisting that the defence of Xuan Loc was vital for the defence of Saigon, his error was in demanding that it be held *at all costs*, instead of allowing for the Saigon forces to fall back, position-by-position, for the defence of the capital itself.

Shortly after the Weyand visit, somebody also arrived on the 'other side' of the line, to the evident satisfaction of *Tuan* and his high-placed comrades.

On the afternoon of 7 April, we were in the middle of a meeting, when a motor-scooter arrived, carrying a rather tall person clad in khaki pants, a blue shirt and army helmet, with a big haversack across his shoulder: Le Duc Tho! We greeted him with the joy that one can imagine. It was his third visit to the South since the start of the resistance 30 years earlier. The other two times, he had made the journey on foot, along unimaginable jungle tracks, winding up and down through the mountains with a bowl of rice and fish as his only ration. And here he was, fresh and in fine fettle, having voyaged this time by plane, car and finally on the back of a motor-scooter.

Very relaxed, he talked to us about the situation back home, the world situation and his impressions of

174

the trip. Just before he left, the Political Bureau and
'Uncle Ton' had said: 'Don't return without Victory!'[8]

The following day, Le Duc Tho briefed *Tuan* and the others
on the Politbureau's decision to set up a special High Command for the campaign to liberate Saigon. *Tuan* was to be
the Military Commander, Pham Hung the Political Commissar; Generals Tran Van Tra and Le Duc Anh the Deputy-
Commanders, and Le Duc Tho, chief of three members of
the Politbureau to help direct the operations.

That Le Duc Tho's journey from Hanoi had taken only a
few days, instead of the six months it had taken for his two
previous north–south journeys, was symbolic of the new
mobility of the revolutionary forces. Ironically, the typical
posture of the Saigon forces, despite their initial vast superiority in mobility, including a total monopoly of air
transport for operational purposes, was that they were now
manoeuvred into situations in which they were constantly
fighting from fixed positions, their backs against the walls or,
sometimes, the sea. The VPA, on the other hand, was literally
running rings around the enemy in terms of mobility and
flexibility. This factor was absolutely decisive during the
weeks ahead, for by the first week of April it was clear to
both sides that they were engaged in a life-and-death race for
time.

Hanoi was informed of the gist of a meeting on 3 April,
held between the commanders of Saigon's élite troops, the
Parachutists, Rangers and Air Force, inspired by General
Weyand's assessments and promises. They had all agreed the
remaining fronts should be held at all costs until the rains
started at the beginning of June. And as from 15 May, the
various training centres could furnish enough replacements to
replace some of the destroyed divisions. By regrouping survivors, rounding up deserters and incorporating new recruits,
four divisions of Rangers could be constituted, three more
regular infantry divisions and eight armoured units. Washington would provide the necessary tanks, armoured cars, artillery and naval support units. (As things turned out Weyand

8. *Dai Thang Hua Xuan*, op cit, p 187.

175

was promising more than the US Congress was prepared to sanction, but Le Duan and Vo Nguyen Giap could not base planning on such assumptions.) Moreover, the rains started falling far earlier than normal, inspiring Le Duc Tho to dash off an anguished poem:

As the sun rises over the Loc Ninh jungle,
I hear the call of the black cuckoo
[harbinger of the rainy season].
All night not a wink of sleep,
Counting the rain drops,
Worried about our soldiers,
Wallowing along endless muddy tracks.
After the tanks, the artillery,
Still no news from either,
Though the Front urgently needs both.
Rain! Please stop,
So the tracks may dry and firm up,
And lead us to our goal.
In this last historic battle,
The first shots are already being fired.[9]

The battle of Xuan Loc had already started. It became inevitable when the first 'Weyand Line' collapsed after Dalat was captured on 4 April. Phan Rang was outflanked and the local people's forces captured many key positions ahead of the advance of the VPA's main forces. The only speed and mobility displayed by the forces manning the 'Weyand Line' was in throwing away weapons and uniforms and heading back to their villages!

As to what happened at Xuan Loc, where Saigon's 18th Division under General Le Minh Dao put up a stubborn defence, I was given a very detailed account from Major Pham Van Con, who headed the local regional forces during the battle. A tough man, with a rocky face, big mouth and strong teeth somewhat reminiscent of Chu Teh, leader of China's Eighth Route Army, Pham Van Con had been

9. Ibid, p 189.

fighting in the area for over twenty years before the decisive battle started. A man of the people if ever there was one!

He explained that Xuan Loc was a highly strategic spot. Enemy troops there were extremely mobile, with plenty of tanks, artillery and motor transport at their disposal for the defence of Saigon. The Saigon forces also boasted of what they called an 'octopus' defence plan. The body of the 'octopus' was Xuan Loc, the tentacles the various roads converging on the city, especially Highway 1, leading west to Bien Hoa, then south to Saigon, and Highway 20, which led south-west from Dalat and joined No. 1 about 20 kms west of Xuan Loc. By controlling these 'tentacles' the army was in a very mobile position and could rush troops quickly to any point under attack.

The main force, as has been mentioned, was the 18th Division, under General Le Minh Dao, who was also overall commander. In addition, he had one regiment of Marines, two brigades of Parachutists, one tank division, three artillery battalions, five battalions of security troops and one regiment of special forces – a platoon for every Xuan Loc hamlet – to repress any people's uprisings. Le Minh Dao also had un-limited support from the nearby Bien Hoa air base. The VPA decided to commit two full divisions, the 341st and 7th, and two regiments of the 6th, in what they knew could be one of the great decisive battles of the war. They had thirty-four artillery pieces, including 120 mm long-range cannon, but their adversaries had 104 pieces including 75, 105 and 155 mm cannon and howitzers. However, in Pham Van Con's own words, 'we counted on overcoming this three-to-one artillery superiority by surprise and our "grabbing the enemy by the belt" tactics'.

Because of excellent co-operation from the local people, *dac cong* units infiltrated Xuan Loc two days before the battle started and were therefore able to examine the enemy's defence system. And with the help of regional and village self-defence forces, the North Vietnamese were able to place the two regiments of the 6th Division into position, so as to interrupt any reinforcements coming from the south-west. It was decided that the 341st and 7th Divisions should

177

move by night, with great secrecy, parallel to Highways 1 and 20, with the intention of making a frontal attack from the east and the north-west. However, they ran into difficulties because, although the initial attack took the Saigon forces by surprise as far as the timing was concerned, their troops were in position. Indeed, knowing the attack would be made at some stage, they fought back tenaciously.

A young officer of the 18th Division, Second-Lieutenant Ung Thanh Phong, whom I was later to meet in a re-education centre for junior officers, told me that at the start of the battle, General Le Minh Dao had addressed the officers to the effect that they must all fight 'to the last man'. They were confident, because of their great concentration of artillery and the air support from the nearby bases of Bien Hoa and Tan Son Nhut (Saigon), that they could prevent any breakthrough. 'If you are captured by the Communists,' said General Dao, 'you will be killed to the last officer and last soldier. Not a man will escape. And the whole of the civilian population will be drowned in a sea of blood. That is why we must fight till the last man.' It was a contributory reason to the fact that the battle for Xuan Loc was the longest and bloodiest of the whole war. For the first three days – long compared with the battles for Buon Me Thuot and Danang – the battle raged without any breakthrough. Part of the reason, it was clear from what Van Tien Dung wrote later, was the lack of co-ordination between regular, regional and guerilla forces, and the local population. Some aspects of secrecy were also broken for the very good reason that the population of Xuan Loc were tipped off on the night preceding the first attack that they would be well advised to visit their relatives in the surrounding villages – which the overwhelming majority of them fortunately did. Pham Van Con's account continued:

We were not getting anywhere and were taking losses. It was decided to switch to a second contingency plan – abandon the frontal attack in favour of encirclement. Our forward elements started pulling back. Le Minh Dao sensed the change in tactics and committed his first big mistake. He called up his 52nd Regiment, which had been

178

kept in reserve to the south-west of the city. It was immediately engaged by our two 6th Division regiments which had been put into position essentially for that. The 52nd Regiment was destroyed – not a single man succeeded in reaching Xuan Loc. Our two regiments then advanced and took up the positions the by then non-existent 52nd Regiment was supposed to occupy. The encirclement of Xuan Loc was thus completed.

One of the major mistakes the Americans – and therefore Saigon – made throughout their whole involvement in Vietnam was to try to judge their adversary's strategies and tactics by their own weights and measures. Thus, according to the information reaching Hanoi's headquarters, Saigon was certain that at least one regiment of the VPA's regular forces would have to be left behind to control every province occupied. The difference between 'occupation' and 'liberation' could not be accepted in Saigon without admitting that the war had been lost in advance. And not only was it not necessary to leave a regiment behind in every province, because the local people took over, but it was always a regiment plus Saigon deserters that the VPA could count on as their forces snow-balled their way south. Certainly the numbers of deserters were never decisive in any engagement, but the Saigon Command's continual misjudgement of the situation was! Once it was realized that Xuan Loc was encircled as completely as Dien Bien Phu had been twenty-one years earlier, orders were given for the defenders to evacuate along Highway 15 to Baria. But all radio communications were monitored, and immediately decoded, thanks to deserters, so that the withdrawal plan was known to the attackers. Orders were therefore given to launch the final assault.

The attack commenced at 10 pm on the night of 21 April with troops advancing from all sides simultaneously. The city soon became an inferno, with planes from Bien Hoa continuously overhead as they had been during the previous eleven days, bombing and rocketing from every level and angle. It was at this stage that the Saigon forces used the seven-ton 'Daisy Cutters' and CBU 55 bombs.[10] Not surprisingly, however, the 'tentacle' system never worked because, with guerillas' and people's support, the VPA were able to achieve local superiority wherever they went. They were also able to draw the Saigon forces away from the centre of Xuan Loc by attacking in the suburbs and to then instruct the *dac cong* to attack in the centre. In desperation Thieu had thrown virtually the entire air force into the battle, but still the VPA's supplies continued to arrive, while Le Minh Dao was horrified to discover that all his supply routes were cut. He had no way of replacing the tremendous expenditure of munitions, and both forces were so tightly engaged, with tanks shooting point-black at each other, that his tactical air power was of little use. For the same roads that were open for VPA supplies were denied to him by the local guerilla forces.

The battle finally ended with an assault on the headquarters of the 18th Division, which was also that of its 43rd Regiment. Part of an archway to what had been an elaborate entrance was the only thing left standing. Even months after the battle it was still a scene of indescribable destruction. Artillery pieces still lying where they had been blown on to their backs; every casemate, every underground bunker, every fire-point and machine-gun nest, had received direct hits. Not a scrap of any building of what was a very big garrison area was left standing. There was still a mass of remnants of machine-gun barrels without stocks, smashed and twisted light arms and hillocks of shell cases. When I remarked on the completeness of the destruction, Major Pham Van Con smiled grimly and said: 'Yes. On the night of the 21st, we managed to get our artillery within 90 ms of the outer perimeter of this headquarters.' Doubtless it was done under the cover of the inferno of exploding bombs and shells and machine-gun fire; but it also seemed one of those miracles which the men of Vo

10. The 'Daisy Cutters' were exploded just above ground level, ostensibly to blast trees and undergrowth out of the jungle for helicopters to land. The CBU 55s discharged scores of small bombs which ejected an aerosol gas. Ignited by built-in fuses, this consumed all the oxygen within several hundred yards, killing everything within the radius of their action. Paul Léandri, the Agence France Presse correspondent, referred to in Chapter 13, had been the first to report the use of CBU 55s in Cambodia.

Nguyen Giap and Van Tien Dung were constantly repeating! 'By 5.20 on the afternoon of 22 April, it was all over,' said Major Pham Van Con. 'We had completely shattered the 18th Division, wiping out to the last man one battalion each of its 43rd and 48th Regiments, not counting the 52nd Regiment destroyed earlier.'

Neither General Le Minh Dao nor his officers 'fought to the last man', although the fact that the battle raged for twelve days and nights testifies to the fact that they fought more stubbornly and more efficiently than any others during the campaign. Some 5500 officers and men were rounded up by local people's forces – and promptly told to go back to their villages once they had laid down their arms. Le Minh Dao, graduate from the US Staff College of Fort Benning, Georgia, and one of the most decorated officers in the Saigon Army, slipped into civilian clothes and gradually made his way to the Mekong delta. One of the first things that impressed him – as also Second-Lieutenant Ung Thang Phong – was that, as distinct from his own troops who went on a rampage of looting and raping once their units were shattered, the VPA men, including regional troops and local guerillas, were disciplined and orderly and immediately established normal, human relations with the civil population. After the fall of Saigon, he registered, like the overwhelming majority of all officers, and was eventually called to report to a re-education centre.

Meanwhile, as Van Tien Dung expressed it: 'silver heads merged with black heads'[11] over the maps of all approaches to Saigon, not to mention over street maps of Saigon itself!

11. *Dai Thang Mua Xuan*, op cit, p 282.

181

CHAPTER 15

TAKING SAIGON

With such a concentration of brain-power and experience at the Loc Ninh headquarters, there were passionate discussions as to whether it was feasible to take Saigon before the rainy season and, if so, how? At one point a cable arrived from Le Duan which left no doubt as to what was expected from the operational commanders. In it he stressed: 'Once launched, the integrated offensive must be carried out with vigour and continuity, striking blow after blow. Attacks in the periphery must be combined with those along the main communication routes, striking straight into the heart of Saigon . . . By combining attacks from the perimeter to the interior and vice versa, conditions will be created for people's uprisings.'[1] He also pointed out that alternatives should be considered in case a turn of events resulted in an extended battle.

Once the main decision was agreed on, there was a constant coming and going of army corps commanders to receive their detailed instructions, the dates by which their units were to be in their jumping-off positions and precise dates by which key objectives were to be secured so that the whole front would move forward in a synchronized pattern.

Haunting the chief planners were the signs of a precocious

1. *Dai Thang Mua Xuan*, op cit, p 192.

rainy season, signs also of diplomatic moves in the world's chief capitals which involved the risk of again losing – as at Geneva in 1954 – the full harvest of military victory. In a pep talk to the High Command and army corps cadres assembled at Loc Ninh, Pham Hung stressed the urgency of 'striking swiftly' and in such a way that 'we will all celebrate Uncle Ho's birthday, 19 May, in Saigon.[2]

It was left to Le Duc Tho to make what would have been the most sensational announcement had Saigon been as well informed of what was being discussed in Loc Ninh as Loc Ninh was informed of what was going on in Saigon and in its various field headquarters:

We are launching our attack against Saigon at the moment when the enemy is at the point of total collapse, has lost his punch. It is we who attack – and into his last hideout. There is no other way out. He will strain every nerve to resist. But . . . he has five divisions, we have fifteen not counting strategic reserves. There is no excuse for us not to win . . .

The American imperialists have absolutely no possibility of making a come-back. As things stand today, all information that we have received excludes the possibilities of renewed intervention. But even if there was such a crazy possibility, they could never reverse the situation and would only suffer even heavier defeats . . . Le Duc Tho insisted on the surprise factor in the attacks and urged the increase of unexpected blows at key points and nerve centres. In a fight, he said, even a very tough man collapses if you hit him at a sensitive point . . .

As for the time factor, he recalled that the rainy season was approaching and that everything must be terminated before it started. If everything was settled during the month of May by the time of 'Uncle Ho's' birthday, the victory would have an added symbolic value.[3]

2. Ibid, p 194.
3 Ibid, pp 194–5.

Accumulating fifteen divisions to deal with Saigon's five was a most astonishing feat. The dream of any military commander is to be able to concentrate overwhelming force against a prime target. That it could be possible was incomprehensible to the Saigon Command, but it represented the essence of the difference between the two types of war that were being fought. It represented the culminating point of Giap's theories of 'People's War'. He could not be caught in the contradiction between dispersal and concentration of his forces because the dispersal part was taken care of by the local people's organizations. As has been mentioned earlier there was no need to leave behind a regiment per province as occupation forces. This would have eaten up a dozen divisions before they reached Saigon if they had been up against a hostile population. On the contrary, they picked up very important reinforcing troops as they raced ahead from all directions to deal the knock-out blow at the solar plexus of the Saigon régime. It was the difference between a fighting force which was based on the aspirations of the overwhelming majority of the Vietnamese people, and another which was the negation of those aspirations. Otherwise how to explain that three-to-one superiority in divisions in favour of one side based almost 2000 kms away in Hanoi and the other defending the supreme citadel of its power?

At a meeting on 7 April, when Pham Hung had asked about the state of supplies, especially munitions, logistics chief Dinh Duc Thien had presented an optimistic statistical report of materials already stocked or 'in the pipe-line', capping his report with the words: 'I can guarantee there's enough to make the enemy tremble for three generations.' *Tuan* remarked that when, as a result, everyone asked for 'a bit more of this or that', Pham Hung amused himself by repeating the formula that invariably provoked outbursts of laughter: 'And I hope that what will be enough to make the enemy tremble for three generations will be speedily delivered.' It is clear, and understandable, that the conference took place in a most optimistic atmosphere. This was in part due to reports which had arrived from the districts and provinces of Zones 8 and 9 (the southern part of the Mekong delta) about the successes which had taken place in the first days of April. Tra Vinh province, for example, announced that it now had five battalions instead of the previous two, and in Rach Gia every village had a minimum of one company of guerillas and one village – in a single day – had raised 200 men to form a supplementary provincial battalion.

It was the same everywhere, with an extremely rapid expansion of units, some armed through new supply routes opened up during the offensive, but a high proportion equipped with freshly captured arms, tanks, trucks and artillery. And at the same time former soldiers or former civilian specialists of the Saigon Army were employed, not only to drive and maintain these different categories of vehicles, but to explain the characteristics of American weapons and equipment, such as cannon and transmitters, so that the VPA could use them effectively.

But it was not only tanks, trucks and artillery that were to be turned against their former owners. On 8 April, an F-5 Phantom fighter-bomber had bombed President Thieu's Independence Palace, and then flown on to land at Phuoc Long in the liberated zone. The pilot, Lieutenant Nguyen Thanh Trung, from the revolutionary province of Ben Tre in the Mekong delta, was the son of a district secretary of the Communist Party who had been executed under the Ngo Dinh Diem régime. He had been deliberately infiltrated into the air force, like so many other militants in every branch of the armed services and administration, and had provided much valuable information about Saigon's deployment of planes. However, *Tuan* felt that he had a better use for Nguyen Thanh Trung, and he received permission from the High Command to immediately transfer the pilot to Danang. Here the young lieutenant initiated pilots in the handling of the numerous A-37s that had fallen into the VPA's hands intact, thus forming a squadron which could be called upon at an appropriate moment.

This decision was later to have dramatic results when Tan Son Nhut airport was bombed and President Ford immediately ordered the evacuation of all Americans from South Vietnam. The 'Vietcong' with an air force, and an American air force at that, was probably the last straw. Especially if it was taken together with everything else that had happened since Lieutenant Trung's defection.

The enormous problem that faced *Tuan*'s command was to move fifteen divisions into place at the right moment for a simultaneous attack straight into the heart of Saigon. There are probably some who will say that it never would have been possible if the Americans had not pulled out. This would be to ignore the 1968 Tet Offensive when – with the Americans at the peak of their strength and in total control of the war under their General William C. Westmoreland – the Vietcong encircled and struck simultaneously at 140 cities, towns and major bases, including Westmoreland's headquarters at Tan Son Nhut airfield and the US Embassy in the heart of Saigon. US air reconnaissance and its famed gadgetry of detection had failed to give any credible warning! Admittedly, this time, there were tanks and heavy artillery involved – in 1968 exclusively shoulder-carried weapons. Five army corps, each comprising three divisions, had to be moved into position to attack in five main prongs from the east, the north, the north-west, the south-west and south. And the maximum of secrecy of movement had to be observed.

One of the great advantages of a tropical climate is that there are twelve hours of dark, every night throughout the year, and the Vietnamese revolutionary forces used this advantage to the full. The order of progression of the various columns was normally the *dac cong* as advance units, who might turn up as beggars, pedlars, or in Saigon uniforms, to contact local organizations, or deal with guards at bridges, river crossings, etc. Hard on their heels came the engineers to repair bridges and perhaps build pontoons, while local guerilla groups would be attacking enemy posts in the area to distract attention. Then came the tanks to deal with any serious resistance, followed by the motorized infantry, artillery and anti-aircraft units. All vehicles and arms were camouflaged with the local vegetation so that at the approach of planes, they could merge into the surrounding jungle, rubber plantations and so on, with only the anti-aircraft units going into action in case the planes really started to attack. Move-

187

ment, like everything else, had to be of the utmost rapidity.

The 1st Army Corps was working on an irrigation project in Ninh Binh province, less than 100 kms south of Hanoi, when it received its marching orders on 25 March. Within fifteen days, it was at its assigned position in the Nam Bo, having covered 1700 kms with all its tanks, artillery and even SAM anti-aircraft missiles. The 2nd Army Corps, which had taken part in the battle for Danang, was advancing along the coast, often fighting by day and moving by night, when it got the order to advance on Bien Hoa, 900 kms to the south-west, within eighteen days. Major rivers, over which the bridges had been destroyed, had to be crossed and major battles fought, including those at Phan Rang and Phan Thiet. With over 2000 vehicles it was a formidable order – but they made it on time.

As the various army corps converged on their jumping-off positions for the final assault, *Tuan* and General Tran Van Tra left the Loc Ninh headquarters to an advanced field headquarters, in what was known throughout the war as the 'Iron Triangle', just east of the Saigon river about 30 kms north of Saigon. Le Duc Tho and Pham Hung remained behind to deal with the overall problems of military, political and economic affairs – not only for the final campaign but also for the administration of the newly liberated areas and preparations for the administration of Saigon.

One of the best-kept secrets was that the VPA kept its advanced headquarters in the southern tip of the 'Iron Triangle' throughout the war. Its rubber plantations, forests and orchards had been completely wiped out, replaced by what the South Vietnamese call 'American grass'. I was repeatedly told that it was sown from planes in many areas after forests had been wiped out by napalm and other forms of chemical warfare, or simply bulldozed out of existence by what were known as 'Roman ploughs'. The theory of local guerilla commanders was that the fast growing 'American grass' was sown to lure them into its excellent cover and then the whole area would be subject to massive napalm-bombing, the main guerilla operations always taking place in the dry season when the grass was suitably inflammable. Napalm had proved relatively ineffective in the damp jungle, so why not replace the jungle and rubber plantations with something which would burn more easily? It was logical to those who saw nature as an enemy which gave shelter and food to guerilla fighters. In any case, in their efforts to create a no-man's-land around Saigon and prevent guerilla advances to the southern capital, the United States commanders and advisers saw to it that natural vegetation, rubber plantations, orchards and market gardens were destroyed to the maximum. They, too, were replaced in vast areas I visited on both sides of the Saigon river, in 1975 and 1977, by 'American grass'.

The 'Iron Triangle' (in Bet Cat district of what was then Thu Dau Mot province) had been the subject of the month-long 'Cedar Falls' operation, one of the bloodiest and most destructive the Americans had carried out – the fullest expression of 'search and destroy' success being reported in the 'body count' figures! It was probably the most bombed, burned, shelled and raked-over area in all of South Vietnam. And yet it was here, at the most climactic moment of the war, that Generals Van Tien Dung and Tran Van Tra decided to establish their headquarters! Le Duc Tho and Pham Hung also turned up a few days later, unable to keep away from the centre of the action.

I asked Ba Huyet, a lean, greying cadre who had help set up and defend the base, how it was possible to hang on? He replied: 'When we got orders to set up a secure base here the first thing we did was to start digging 30 kms of underground tunnels. It was in 1960. Not only was this one of our closest outposts to Saigon, but it was our advanced command post throughout the war. The Americans knew something was going on here, but they were not sure what.'

In general, it was difficult to completely keep secrets from the Americans, which would explain the continual 'search and destroy' raids in the area. But, despite the large military operations in 1965, 1969 and 1970, with smaller ones in between, the local guerillas managed to defend themselves by utilizing the tunnel and above-ground block-house systems effectively, constantly taking the Americans by surprise.

It was only by talking with cadres like Ba Huyet, delving

deep into how they had lived and fought, many of them for thirty years without any let-up, that one could understand the spirit which made possible 30 April 1975. 'Living in underground tunnels, and with no means of production, how did you eat?' I asked. He replied: 'We had our contacts within the "strategic hamlets" and the comrades there always managed to put something aside for us. We were always "fish in the sea" even if most of our sea was locked up in the "strategic hamlets". And we always managed to grow a bit of food – at least some manioc. It was not only armed struggle we were waging but political struggle also and because of that our contact with the people was always maintained.'

I then asked about the role of the 'Iron Triangle' veterans during the final offensive, apart from providing the advanced headquarters and protecting it. This time it was Tran Ngoc Khanh, Vice-President of the People's Committee of Song Be province (now a fusion of the former provinces of Thu Dau Mot, Phuoc Long, Binh Long and the Di An district of Tu Duc province), who replied by saying that from the start of the attack on Buon Me Thuot, the main task, as elsewhere for local guerillas, was to pin down the enemy's regular troops by harassing actions. He went on: 'Later as things developed, we intensified these actions to ensure that troops from here could not move to reinforce Saigon, at the same time as ensuring that when the moment came, our own regular forces could pass straight on through without any interference. Once the final offensive was launched we contributed to the destruction of the enemy's 5th Division, finally occupying their headquarters and liberating Ben Cat district with our local guerillas and regional troops.'

One of *Tuan*'s major problems on the eve of leaving the Loc Ninh base, and after receiving reassuring reports that the converging attack columns were moving more or less to plan, was how to put the Tan Son Nhut airport out of action. In order to do this, he had to move his 130 mm cannon to within at least 20 kms of the air strips. After a careful study of the maps and consultation with local commanders, he gave orders for the seizure of the district centre of Nuoc Trong, just 20 kms by shell-flight south-east of Tan Son Nhut, by 27 or 28 April at the latest. The only factor which could seriously interrupt the final phase of the movement towards the formidable inner Saigon defence circle, defended by the capital's five crack divisions, was massive intervention by planes based within that circle. On 25 April, *Tuan* was informed by Colonel Hoang Ngoc Dieu, the Deputy Commander of the air force, that Lieutenant Nguyen Thanh Trung had worked well and that pilots from Hanoi had quickly familiarized themselves with handling the captured A-37s. Some of these had now been transferred to a network of bases just to the north of Phan Rang. *Tuan* knew that speed was of the essence, because the first storms of the rainy season had just broken out, and he made it clear to Hoang Ngoc Dieu that Tan Son Nhut airport was to be attacked within the next two or three days. *Tuan* instructed Hoang Ngoc Dieu to arrange for planes, pilots and mechanics to be moved from Danang to Phan Rang.

At dawn on the following day, with the rains still pelting down, *Tuan* left for his 'Iron Triangle' headquarters. He describes it as a 'former base of our Saigon commandos . . . from where young men and women from our assault sections had carried out particularly devastating raids right into the heart of Saigon. In the collection of makeshift huts, open to the four winds, the roofs offered large views of cloud and sky . . .'[4] The opening shots of the final battle were fired at 5 pm that same day, 26 April, by units of two army corps advancing from the east. It was a real attack, but also a diversionary one to confirm the belief of the Saigon Command that the main attack would be from that direction. It was an obvious assumption. From a tactical viewpoint it was necessary in order to get the troops and equipment across the very wide and fast flowing Dong Nai and Saigon rivers.

On the morning of the 27th, General Di Thien Tich of the veteran southern 9th Division – the growth of which I had observed during my four visits to the South from the time autonomous companies started to fuse into battalions in 1963–4 – received orders to transfer his division from its current operational area, about 70 kms north-east of Saigon, to an area about 20 kms south-west of the capital by the

4. Ibid, p 264.

191

night of the 29th, ready to dash into Saigon before dawn the following day. It meant infiltrating the enemy's most densely concentrated defence positions while still preserving secrecy. Later I was to ask him how he managed this extraordinary feat:

For maximum security we broke up into battalion- and company-sized units, heading towards the Vam Co river, marching by night at maximum speed. For a start, we left the armour and artillery behind. We hid by day on the 28th in the jungle and marched again all night. Hiding up by day on the 29th was difficult because it was open country. But our men were very disciplined, covering themselves with grass and straw and lying in the furrows of ploughed land. Plenty of peasants saw us. There were no betrayals. Crossing the very wide Vam Co [river] was through 40 to 50 kms of strong enemy defences. Another big obstacle was crossing the 20 km wide Bien Loc swamp. But it had been arranged that there would be lots of guerilla activity in the areas through which we had to pass. Also we had the codes and names of enemy officers in the various posts so we hooked our field telephones on their lines, assuring that everything was 'all quiet' in the places where we wanted to cross the river, or to infiltrate through a group of their block-houses. At that stage the rank and file puppet troops and junior officers were not looking for much trouble anyway.

At some of the river crossings we left small groups to help the armour and artillery units following along behind. Local guerillas led us to the best spots to get the heavy weapons across the swamp. Once we got to the Duc Hua area things were easier. We knew the terrain, the people knew us. We had opened the way to Saigon via this route during the 1968 Tet offensive . . .[5]

General Di Thien Tich did not manage to move all his heavy weapons across the swamp – some sank so deep into

5. Wilfred Burchett *Grasshoppers and Elephants* (New York, 1977), pp 48–9.

the mud that they had to be blown up – but he did place his forces in position for the dawn attack on the 30th. His action was only one small piece of the vast military mosaic being fitted together by master hands in the area surrounding Saigon during the final hours before the assault was launched. Incredible as it was, the Saigon Command had no inkling of the vast scale of the military mechanism which was gradually closing in. General Tich's 9th Division was only the shock force of the 232nd Army Group, which included the 24th and 88th autonomous Regiments which were also to erupt into Saigon from the seemingly impassable southern sector.

The overall VPA plan was to use its numerical superiority to encircle and isolate all the units manning the outer defences of Saigon, while their crack units dashed straight ahead with maximum speed to capture the city's main military and administrative centres. Each army corps had one élite division charged with this special task of racing direct to a key objective, while the rest of the corps figuratively pinned the enemy's arms behind his back. But the type of obstacles that had to be overcome can be judged from the reports pouring into *Tuan*'s headquarters as the final touches were being put to the battle plans.

The 304th Division which had fired the first shots on the afternoon of the 26th had quickly seized a tank school and part of the Nuoc Trong naval base, but the defenders, reinforced by cadets from the Thu Duc Military Academy, had fought back fiercely in a series of counter-attacks that had raged all night and throughout the whole day of the 27th under a blazing sun. A special truck unit had to be sent to bring drinking water to the attackers. As they had to fight a daytime battle they were held up by heavy air attacks which made neutralization of the Tan Son Nhut and Bien Hoa air bases all the more urgent. By the morning of the 28th, resistance had been overcome and the 304th, together with the 325th and 3rd Divisions of the 2nd Army Corps were advancing again. Along Highway 1, the 4th Corps had also encountered serious resistance in advancing towards Bien Hoa, 25 kms north of Saigon. *Tuan* notes that: 'For the first time in the Indochina war a series of barriers and anti-tank ditches formed part of the fortified line.' He goes on:

> Our *dac cong* however had secured the bridges of Rach Chiec, Rach Cat, Ghenh and the [all-important] auto-route bridge over the Saigon river, and were awaiting the arrival of our regulars. The enemy launched one counter-attack after another. Furious battles took place for the Rach Cu bridge and for the Bien Hoa–Saigon autoroute bridge over the Dong Nai [a very vital bridge over the wide Dong Nai river] which was taken and retaken several times in bitter hand-to-hand fighting before remaining in our hands. By such feats of arms, our *dac cong* opened the way to Saigon to our regular troops.
>
> During this time our long-range artillery stationed at Hieu Liem had paralysed the Bien Hoa air base. The enemy was obliged to transfer its planes to Tan Son Nhut and on the afternoon of 28 April, the headquarters of its 3rd Army Corps abandoned Bien Hoa for Go Vap [3 kms east of Tan Son Nhut]. Soon after a cadre from the Operations Bureau came into my office with a report which, by the look on his face, could only mean good news.
>
> 'At 3.40 pm,' he said, 'a squadron of five A-37s, piloted by our men, guided by Nguyen Thanh Trung, has taken off from Thanh Son [Phan Rang] for a raid on Tan Son Nhut.'
>
> At last for the first time in the history of our armed forces a truly combined operation was taking place. This event of first-class importance could not but have a great influence on the development of the campaign. I remembered my words to Hoang Ngoc Dieu three days earlier . . . The head of the air force, Le Van Tri, had personally gone to Thanh Son to keep an eye on things and . . .
>
> When our planes penetrated the Tan Son Nhut air space, the control tower was astonished at their presence: 'A-37s, to what squadron do you belong?'
>
> The reply of our pilots, 'A Made in the USA Squadron', was accompanied by sticks of bombs dropped on planes

parked on the tarmac. The explosions rocked Saigon and thick columns of smoke billowed up from the airfield. This daring raid which destroyed a number of planes intended for evacuation purposes only added to the general panic . . .[6]

Very few people on either side knew what had really happened. *Tuan* noted that even in his own headquarters those who did not need to be 'in the know' believed it was either part of an air force attempted *coup d'état*, or another version of Nguyen Thanh Trung's lone-handed effort just twenty days before. The loss of the Bien Hoa and Tan Son Nhut air bases, together with another substantial quantity of planes at the latter, greatly diminished Saigon's use of air power on which the defence capacity of the city was largely based.

To the north of the city the VPA's 1st Corps had seized a section of Highway 13, just north of Thu Dau Mot, sufficient for its shock force to speed on to the capital. The 3rd Army Corps had done the same on Highway 22 to the north-west; and a *dac cong* unit, together with the Gia Dinh regional troops, had even managed to seize a section of the perimeter highway which surrounds Saigon and opened a breach in the defence barrier protecting Tan Son Nhut airport from the north. In the south, the 9th Division was moving into place and in the south-west local forces had completely cut Highway 4 which linked the Mekong delta with Saigon.

On the political front, Nguyen Van Thieu had resigned on 21 April and fled to Taiwan, five days later, with sixteen tons of baggage, after bitterly accusing Washington of 'treachery'. His successor, the ultra-reactionary former Vice-President Tran Van Huong, had displayed the same mad sense of unreality as Thieu and, like Hitler in his bunker as Soviet forces were closing in on Berlin in May 1945, was still placing his faith in 'miracle weapons'. With fifteen VPA divisions closing in on Saigon and scores of *dac cong* and other armed units inside the city itself, Tran Van Huong addressed the National Assembly: 'The supposed ten Vietcong divisions around Sai-

6. *Dai Thang Mua Xuan*, op cit, pp 270-1.

195

gon! It's a bluff, a bogey invented by the opposition! . . .
Where could the Vietcong have fished up ten divisions? And
if they did exist our air force would obliterate them with CBU
bombs. A single CBU could wipe out a whole division!'[7] On
28 April Tran Van Huong was replaced by General Duong
Van 'Big' Minh, who immediately started talking of negotiations.

In a corner of Tan Son Nhut airport, in what was known as
Camp Davis, was the North Vietnamese delegation to the
Joint Military Commission, set up within the framework of
the 1973 Paris Agreement. From the moment of their arrival,
the members had been treated virtually as prisoners, their
headquarters surrounded with barbed wire, subject to all
sorts of provocations, including periodic cutting off of their
water and electricity supply and communications. Suddenly
they became the focus of a flurry of diplomatic attention.
Late on the night of the 28th, three representatives of the 'Big'
Minh administration arrived to suggest negotiations. They
were politely received and their proposal politely rejected.
When they were about to leave, they were cordially invited to
stay the night in view of the artillery bombardment. This
they did. As they did not return, four more came and the
same thing happened. One of the suggestions was that a
delegation be sent to Hanoi to negotiate. US Ambassador
Graham Martin asked for a meeting. It was all far too late.
The by now inevitable had to happen. While a massive
evacuation air-lift went into operation on the 29th, including
the departure of Ambassador Martin, the five army corps
completed their movements into position.

Starting from before dawn on the morning of the 30th,
Tuan describes the action:

On our map, like petals of the lotus flower our five
columns blossomed into life. The 1st Army Corps occupied the General Staff Headquarters and those of the
various branches of the armed forces. The 3rd Corps
seized Tan Son Nhut where it effected a junction with a
'column' which was already on the spot – our military
7. Ibid, p 249.

196

delegation at Camp Davis. The reunion was both pic-
turesque and moving! The 4th Corps installed itself at
the Ministry of Defence, the Bach Dang port and the
Radio. Group 232 (of which the 9th Division was the
shock force) controlled the Headquarters of the 'Special
Saigon Military Zone' and the Police Headquarters.
The 2nd Corps took over the 'Independence Palace' . . .
At 11.30 am the flag of the revolution floated over the
'Independence Palace', which had by then become the
point of convergence of all our columns. At the Headquarters, we were leaning over the radios following the
news. It was thus we heard Duong Van Minh announce
unconditional surrender. Saigon entirely liberated!
Victory, total Victory! The whole headquarters started
jumping and yelling with joy. Hugs, congratulations,
applause, great gusts of laughter . . . Le Duc Tho and
Pham Hung took me in their arms as did everyone else
present. We were almost speechless. We didn't know
what to say, overcome with happiness. I lit a cigarette.[8]

Obviously it was not just a question of red and blue flags
being moved on a street map of Saigon. There were some very
fierce battles, mainly at key street intersections. One was at
the Bay Hien crossroads where seven streets come together
less than a mile from the heart of Saigon. The 9th Division's
1st (Binh Gia) Regiment had fought its way through to there
by 7 am, just two hours after leaving its jumping-off point.
Their advance was held up for forty minutes by troops fighting
back from long-prepared positions, reinforced-concrete underground bunkers and heavy machine-guns covering all seven
approaches. Planes joined in to bomb and strafe, but they
were handicapped by having to operate out of Can Tho airport, 130 kms south-west of Saigon. It was at the Bay Hien
crossroads that the 9th Division took its heaviest casualties
in the whole action – over forty killed and wounded. Its
operations officer, Captain Buy Huy, who took part in the
action, told me how it ended:

8. Ibid, p 300.

197

At a critical stage, 20 enemy tanks joined in, but the people were out in mass by then. They just encircled those tanks, clambered all over them, telling the crews they were going to die uselessly. The crews couldn't even aim their guns. So they gave up – surrendered. The local residents started to look after our wounded immediately, although there were bullets flying in all directions.[9]

Nothing, however, could hold up the weight and momentum of the advance and the crashing down of the gates of the Independence Palace.

Thirty years of bitter war and terrible destruction of the works of man and nature had thus ended. What next? One could expect that developments would follow with the same dash and speed as the last offensive – and they did. Preparations for elections to unify the country went ahead at full speed. These included a census to prepare the electoral rolls. To the surprise of everyone, it was found that the population of the South was almost exactly that of the North, whereas it had generally been considered that the South had several million less than the North. The total turned out to be almost 50 million. Elections were held on 25 April 1976 to an All Vietnam National Assembly, represented by 249 deputies from the North, 243 from the South. Their first task was to abolish the North–South concept by voting for the establishment of the Socialist Republic of Vietnam, with Hanoi as its capital, Ton Duc Thang as its President and Pham Van Dong, its Prime Minister. Vo Nguyen Giap retained his post as Defence Minister and Commander-in-Chief of the Armed Forces but, significantly, became Deputy Prime Minister in charge of Science and Technology, the key ministry charged with finding short cuts along the road to develop Vietnam as a modern, industrial-agricultural state. His view of the future was contained in a report on science and technology presented to the 4th Congress of the Vietnam Communist Party, held in Hanoi in December 1966. At the end of a detailed analysis of the tasks ahead, with much stress on the role that Man, with his illimitable creative capacities must play and the

9. *Grasshoppers and Elephants*, op cit, p 43.

198

absolute necessity of restoring and protecting Nature, he concluded:

'The industrialization of our country will be successfully carried out and a new Vietnam, with a modern industrial and agricultural structure, will be born. Our Vietnamese landscape will be transformed and future generations will live a happy and civilized life finally able to enjoy the beauties of this landscape, under a clear sky and pure atmosphere, with its generous mountains and seas, its luxuriant vegetation and beautiful summer nights.'

Thus spoke soldier-poet Giap, the practical visionary entrusted with a key role in ensuring that what is handed on to future generations corresponds to the words of Ho Chi Minh in his Testament that, when the war ended: 'We will build our country ten times more beautiful.'

SELECT BIBLIOGRAPHY

Anthologie de la Littérature Vietnamienne (Editions en Langues Etrangères; Hanoi, 1973), 3 vols.

Burchett, Wilfred. *Grasshoppers and Elephants* (Urizen Books; New York, 1977).

Chesneaux, Jean. *Contribution à l'Histoire de la Nation Vietnamienne* (Editions Sociales; Paris, 1955).

Devillers, Philippe. *Histoire du Vietnam de 1940–52* (Editions de Seuil; Paris, 1952).

Ho Chi Minh. *Oeuvres Choisies du Président Ho Chi Minh* (Editions en Langues Etrangères; Hanoi, 1960–2), 4 vols.

——. *Carnet de Prison* (Editions en Langues Etrangères; Hanoi, 1966).

——. *Le Procès de la Colonialisation Française* (Librairie de Travail; Paris, 1925).

Hoi Thanh and Than Tinh (eds). *Souvenirs sur Ho Chi Minh* (Editions en Langues Etrangères; Hanoi, 1965).

Huynh Khac Dung. *L'Enseignement dans l'Ancien Vietnam* (France-Asie; Saigon, 1952).

Lacouture, Jean. *Ho Chi Minh* (Allen Lane; London, 1968).

Mus, Paul. *Vietnam, Sociologie d'une Guerre* (Editions de Seuil; Paris, 1952).

Pattu, Léopold. *Histoire de l'Expedition de Cochi–Chine en 1861*) Librairie L. Hachette et Cie; Paris, 1864).

201

Van Tien Dung. *Dai Thang Mua Xuan* (The Spring Offensive), (People's Army Publishing House; Hanoi, 1976).

Vo Nguyen Giap. *Guerre du Peuple, Armée du Peuple* (Editions en Langues Etrangères; Hanoi, 1961).

——. *Armement des Masses Révolutionnaires, Edification de l'Armée du Peuple* (Editions en Langues Etrangères; Hanoi, 1974).

Vo Nguyen Giap and Tryong Chinh. *Van De Dan Cay* (The Peasant Problem) (Duc Cuong Publishing House; Hanoi, 1937–8). Published in two volumes under the pseudonyms of Van Dinh and Qua Ninh.

Vietnam: A Historical Sketch (Foreign Languages Publishing House; Hanoi, 1974).

Vietnamese Women. Vietnamese Studies, No. 10, *Xunhasaba*, (Hanoi, 1966).

202

INDEX

British, 90, 92; communist party, 101
Bronze Age, 14
Bronzes, Dong Son, 13; 14
Buddhism, 63, 78
Bui Lam, 104
Buon Ho, 155
Buon Me Thut, 139, 142–60, 166, 178
Burma, 92, 136
Buy Huy, Captain, 197

Cambodia, 9, 14, 18, 24, 78, 117, 135–6, 139, 157, 159
Cambodians (Khmers), 8
Camp Davis, 196–7
Cam Ranh, 159
Canada, 124
Canals, 8
Can Tho airport, 197
Canton, 103–4, 106–7, 112
Cao Bang province, 117–20, 122, 144
Cao Van Vien, General, 161
Card, 145
Carlton Hotel, 99
Castries De, Colonel, 110
Catholicism, 79, 144, 168
Catholic missionaries, 56
Central America, 7
Central Highlands, 11, 90, 129, 133–4, 139, 141–2, 144, 146, 150, 157–8, 163–6, 168, 171, 174
Central Intelligence Agency (CIA), 165
Central Military Committee, 123, 138–9, 144, 155, 163
Central Vietnam, 24
Champa Kingdom, 27–8, 30, 51
Chams, 8–9, 26
Chateaubriand, 88
Chen Lung, Emperor, 54
Chesneaux, Jean, 12
Chiang Kai-Shek, 107, 116, 118
Chien, 128, 152, 155, 157, 164–5, 167–9
Chi Lann, 37
China, 8–9; bronzes, 14; 18, 23; revolution, 24; 28, 35; three-tier military system, 46, 52, 63–4; jail, 69, 111–13, 116–18; treaty with France (May 1884), 84–6; Ho Chi Minh, 103, 107, 124, 135–6; military supplies, 172
Chinese, 1–2; agriculture, 7; invaders, 9; expansion, 15–18; defeat, 19–20, 23; forces, 37, 46; 73, 97; classics, 136–7
Ch'in dynasty, 18
Ch'ing dynasty, 22, 55, 84, 95
Cholon Chinese, 91
Chou En-Lai, 107, 173
Christian religion, 63–4, 85–6
Chu Huy Man, General, 141, 169, 171
Chungking, 117, 136
Chu Teh, 176
Chu Van Tan, 123
Clausewitz, Karl von, 30
Coastal plains, 133, 146, 158–9, 161–2, 165, 174
Cochin-Chine, Upper and Lower, 51, 53, 55, 62, 87
Coffee, 75, 90

Colani, Madeline, 7
Co Loa, ruins of, 12, 14; base for army of King An Duong, 18
Colonialism, western, 56
Columbus, Christopher, 46
Comintern, 103, 107
Communist party, 137
Communist party of Britain, 101
Communist party of France, 103, 115
Communist party of Indochina, 104, 113
Compulsory military service, 23–4
Confucianism, 20–1, 47, 62–4, 66–71, 78–9, 84–5, 88
Cong Hoa military hospital, 171
Con Son island, 61
Corvée (forced unpaid labour), 66, 97
Cromwell, Oliver, 64
Cultural relics, destroyed by invaders, 9

Dac cong, 145, 147, 153–4, 163, 166, 180, 194–5
Dac Lac province, 144, 151–2
Dai (great) Viet, 26–8, 30
Dakar, 98
Dalat, 176
Danang, 41, 61, 76, 143, 161, 166–71, 178, 186, 188, 191
Dang Van Quang, General, 161
Decoration of bronze drums, 14
Destruction of the Mongol fleet, 32
De Tham, 95
Di An district, 190
Dien Bien Phu, 42, 105, 109–11, 122, 138, 145, 149, 179
Dien Duc Thien, 156, 185
Dinh-Le rulers, 25
Dinh Tien Hoang, 55
Disease, tropical, 28
Di Thien Tich, General, 191–2
Djakarta, 173
Do Ban, 53
Domestication, 8
Dong Hoi, wall, 48, 51–2, 81; fishing port, 127, 172
Dong Khanh, King, 78
Dong Nai river, 191, 194
Dong Si Nguyen, General, 134
Dong Son civilization, 12–13
Don Luan, 130
Doumer, Paul, Governor-General, 87
Draft agreement, 131
Duc Hua, 192
Duc Phong, 130
Dutch colonies, 100
Duong Van (Big) Minh, 196–7
Dykes, 8, 45

East China Sea, 27
Education, 64–5, 85–90, 98
Eighth Conference of the Party's Central Committee (May 1941), 117
Eighth Route Army, 116
Egypt, 14
Elections, 198
Elephants, use of, 38, 55, 157

204

Metal age, 13
Migratory tribes, 5
Mikado, land of, 97
Military machine, US, 43
Military training, universal, 23–4, 46
Ming dynasty, 22, 33; troops, 34, 36–41, 55, 69, 95
Missionaries, Catholic, 56, 78
Mongolia, 27
Mongolian People's Republic, 128
Mongols, 2, 9, 22–3; invasion and defeat of, 27–31, 55, 73, 76
Montagnards, 134, 139, 153–4, 161
Montesquieu, 89
Moscow, 44, 107, 156
Muong, 28
Muskets, 120, 122
My Chanh river, 167

Nam Bo, 172, 188
Nangan, 122
Nan-ning, 118
Napalm, 188–9
Napoleon, 111
Napoleon III, 62
National Council of National Reconciliation and Concord, 131
National Council of Scientific Research (CNSR), 5
National Liberation Front of South Vietnam, 123
National Museum, Hanoi, 14
Nature, need to restore and protect, 199
Negotiations, Paris (May 1968–Jan 1973), 124
Neolithic period, 8–9, 13
New Caledonia, 75
New Fourth Army, 116
New Man, 69
'New World', 46
Nghe An province, 7, 30, 34, 54–5, 95–6; Soviet, 113
Ngoc Han, 54
Ngo Dinh Diem, 123, 186
Ngo Quang Truong, General, 167, 170
Ngo Quen, defeated Chinese (938). 19–29; 23, 25, 32
Ngo Tuan, General, 26
Nguyen Ai Quoc (Ho Chi Minh), 93, 101–2, 104, 106–7, 112–13, 115–17
Nguyen Anh, 53–6, 61–2, 66, 68; 70
Nguyen Chon, Colonel, 170
Nguyen Dinh Thi, 21, 73–6
Nguyen dynasty, 24; 19th century, 47–8, 56, 77–8, 84, 90
Nguyen Du, 69, 71, 95
Nguyen Hue, 48–50, 52–5, 59, 77, 102
Nguyen Khac Vien, Dr, 24, 63, 77, 88
Nguyen lords, 51–3
Nguyen Lu, 52, 55–6
Nguyen Luong Bang, 98, 106
Nguyen Nhac, 52–3, 56
Nguyen Sinh Cung (Ho Chi Minh), 93
Nguyen Sinh Sac, Dr, 67, 86, 95–7
Nguyen Tat Thanh (Ho Chi Minh), 93, 96–7
Nguyen Thanh Trung, Lieutenant, 186, 194

Nguyen Thi Dinh, Deputy Commander-in-Chief, 19
Nguyen Thi Hang, 20
Nguyen Trai, 34–43, 45–6, 67, 69, 76, 109, 172
Nguyen Van Thieu, President, 124–5, 129–30, 140, 153, 156, 158, 161, 163–4, 168, 180, 195
Nguyen Van Tong, 78
Nguyen Van Troi, 80
Nha Trang, 146, 159
Nhu Quyet river, 26
Ninh Binh province, 188
Nixon, Richard, President, 132
Non Nuoc, 170
Northern China, 27
Northern Vietnam, 2, 10–11, 41–2, 92, 122, 124, 136, 141, 144, 177, 198
Nui Bong, 166
Nui (Mount) Do, 6
Nui Nghe, 166
Nung ethnic minority, 123
Nuoc Man air base, 170
Nuoc Trong, 190

Omar, 31–2
Operation Ho Chi Minh, 57
Operation 275, 144
Opium, 91
Origin of Vietnamese people, 5–15

Pac Bo Conference, 117
Palaeolithic Society, 6–7
Pallu, Léopold, 83
Paris Commune (1871), 78
Paris peace talks, 32, 69; agreement, 124–5, 127, 129, 132, 196
Pathet Lao, 135
P. C. Lin (Ho Chi Minh), 115
Peasantry, historical role, 49; nature of, 74, 92–3
Peking, Man, 5; 27–8, 33, 44, 84, 105, 112
Pentagon, 137, 143
Peoples' Anti-Corruption Movement, 153
People's Army of Vietnam (VPA), 17, 22, 32, 45, 58
People's War, 26, 32, 41–3, 184
Permanent Bureau of the Politbureau, 143
Petition of Hoang Dieu, 79–80
Petition to France, 100
Pham Day Tat, Colonel, 161
Pham Hong Thai, 103
Pham¹Hung, 57, 141, 171–2, 175, 185, 188–9
Pham Huy Thong, Professor, 5–9, 13–15
Pham Ngh Lao, General, 32, 132
Pham Ngoc Thach, 110–11
Pham Van Con, Major, 176–7, 180–1
Pham Van Dong, Prime Minister, 3, 11, 106–7, 112–13, 115–19, 127, 129, 141, 171, 178, 198
Pham Van Phu, General, 161
Phan Boi Chau, Dr, 96–7, 102, 106–7, 112, 114
Phan Chu Tinh, 107, 112

208

Sun Tzu, General, 30
Sun Yat Sen, 103, 107
Superior Man, 69
Support committee, 171
Szechuan province, 27

Tactic against invasion fleets, 23
T'ai P'ing peasant rebellion, 53
Tai wan, 195
Tam Ky, 168, 170
Tam Tam Xa (Union of Hearts), 103
Tang dynasty, 23
Tanks, 148, 150, 187
Tan Son Nhut airport (Saigon), 178,
    186–7, 190–1, 194–6
Tan Viet (Revolutionary Association of
    Annam), 112–13
Taoism, 78
Task Force A-75, 136
Taxes, 90–1
Tay Au principality, 11
Tay Ninh province, 129–30, 164
Tay Nguyen, 105
Tay Son insurrection, 49, 52–4, 61, 71, 84
Tay Tinh, 158
Teachers, French, 5
Teak, 90
Temple of Literature, 63, 67
Ten States period (907–960), 20
Testament of Ho Chi Minh, 106, 199
Tet (Lunar New Year's Day), 110;
    offensive by NLF (1968), 124, 128–9, 145,
    187, 192
Thanh Giong, boy prodigy, 17
Thanh Hoa province, 6; coast, 12–13; 20,
    30, 34, 95
Thanh Long (Hanoi) citadel, 21, 24, 28, 34,
    48, 54–6
Thanh Nien, 112
Thanh Son, 194
Third Force, 131
Thoat Hoan, 31
Thoi Tu, 38
Three categories of troops, 24–5, 46
Thu Dau Mot, province, 189–90, 195
Thuy Tinh, water genie, 10–11, 17
Tien Phuoc, 170
Timur Khan, 32
Toa Do, General, 30
Toghan, General, 30–2
Tolstoy, Leo, 102
Tools, stone, 6–8
Ton Duc Thang, President, 3, 98, 112–13,
    132, 198
Ton King, 7, 86–7
Tong Minh Phuong, 122
Ton Tan Thuyet, 78
Toulon, 98
Tourine, 62
Tours Congress (25–30 December 1920),
    101
Tra Lan, 37
Tran Binh Trong, General, 30
Tran Dang Ninh, 136
Tran Di Ai, 28
Tran dynasty, 26, 32–3, 46, 76

Tran Hung Dao, 29, 55, 76
Tran Hung Dao, 29–31, 40, 132
Tran Hung Dao platoon, 111
Tran Nhan Ton, King, 29–33
Tran Ngoc Khanh, 190
Tran Quang Khai, General, 30
Tran Quoc Tuan, 29
Tran rulers, 28
Tran Thien Khiem, Premier General, 161
Tran Te Xuong, 87
Tran Tuu Thanh, Father, 153–4
Tran Van Huong, Vice-President, 195–6
Tran Van Tra, General, 171, 175, 188–9
Tran Va Tra, General, 141
Tra Vinh province, 186
Treaty signed with French (28 November
    1787), 61
Trieu Thi Trinh (Dame Trieu), 19
Trieu Quang Phuc, 21–2
Trinh Minh The bridge, 171
Trinh régime, 48, 51–3
Tri-Thien region, 166, 168
'Troops of the Just Cause', 50, 53, 77, 166
Troung Chinh, 113–14, 141, 145
Trung Nhi, 19
Trung sisters, 19, 55
Trung Trac, 19
Truong Dinh, Commander-in-Chief,
    Pacifier of the French, 84
Truong Han Sieu, 63
Truong Son mountains, 135
Truong Tan, 80
Tsarist Russia, 96, 102
Tsing Si, 116–18
Tuan, 127–8, 130, 134, 145–7, 151–2, 155–8,
    160, 162–7, 169, 171–2, 174–5, 185–6, 188,
    190–1, 193–4
Tu Duc, King, 77, 79, 84; province, 190
Tu Nguyen, 172
Tuy Hoa, 142, 160

US Air Force, 7, 124, 149
US Congress, 176
US Embassy, 187
US Staff College of Fort Benning, Georgia,
    181
US troops, 41–2, 123
Ung Thanh Phong, Second-Lieutenant, 178,
    181
United States, 11; key to defeat, 22;
    –Saigon régime war (1960–75), 26; 36;
    resistance to, 74, 80; Ho Chi Minh, 98;
    invasion of Laos, 111; confounded, 120;
    Geneva Convention, 122; confronted,
    124; 140–2, 161
Unit, 59, 134–6

Vam Co river, 192
Van De Can Cay (The Peasant Problem),
    114
Van Dinh (Vo Nguyen Giap), 114
Vanguard Unit to Advance Southward
    formed, 119
Van Lang, 10